THE BAILIFF OF BLACKMOOR

Luxulyan Church Tower. The 1305 Stannary Charter was kept here for centuries. It was secured in a coffer with eight locks.

Photograph *Herbert Hughes, Royal Institution of Cornwall*

The

Bailiff of Blackmoor
1586

Thomas Beare

An examination of the history, laws and customs
of medieval and sixteenth century tinners.

Transcribed and Edited by
J.A. Buckley, B.A.(Hons.), M.Phil., M.C.S.M., F.R.Hist.S.

Penhellick

Publications

First published by Penhellick Publications, Camborne, Cornwall
© J.A. Buckley 1994

ISBN 1 871 678 01 3
(Hard back)

ISBN 1 871 678 06 4
(Soft back)

To
Henry Leslie Douch
In acknowledgment of his immense
contribution of Cornish history research
of so many years

CONTENTS & LIST OF ILLUSTRATIONS

ACKNOWLEDGMENTS

During the eight years that it has taken to bring this book to fruition I have been helped by a great many people. Bryan Earl and I conceived the project during our researches into early tin dressing and blowing techniques, when we realised that despite the wealth of relevant information in Harleian Manuscript 6380, it was not available to read except in its original form. Upon enquiring of Mr Leslie Douch, then curator of the County Museum, Truro, about a transcription of the manuscript we were informed that although he had transcribed it some twenty years before, his version had been loaned to A.K.H. Jenkin and had not been seen since. Having encouraged me to get started, Mr Douch then helped me to translate many semi-legible words, and then read through the whole transcription and made many corrections and useful comments. Bryan Earl's contribution to this book is immeasurable. He has assisted me at every juncture and encouraged me constantly. The late Professor Ronnie Tylecote and his wife Elizabeth also were a source of encouragement during the early period of work.

Once the book was transcribed and checked through it was decided that the several Latin pages should be translated into English. Mr. Robert Petre, of the Cornwall Record Office, was approached to carry out this task. His skillful translation, using my less-than-perfect transcription, makes available a significant proportion of the book. I am grateful to him for his tireless efforts, especially after several pages were lost in the post and had to be re-translated.

Among those individuals who have answered specific questions, helped me locate obscure sources, encouraged me with advice, or offered explanations on various points that came up whilst transcribing the text (or understanding it) are Clive Carter, Tom Greeves, Michael Tangye, Len Truran, David Thomas and Joe Thomas, all of whom have a deep understanding of aspects of Cornish mining or social history.

As with all works of this type the efforts of Christine North's staff at the Cornwall Record Office, Angela Broom, at the RIC Library and Terry Knight and his staff at Redruth Local Studies Library, have been crucial.

It would be impossible to name all those who have helped produce this book, but among those whom I must thank are Jennie Hinton, Emma Priestly and Karla Riekstins, all of South Crofty Mine, who have helped me with many tasks including typing, checking the index and copying. I must also thank Emma Priestly for the map, based on one of Norden's, and Bryan Earl for the photographs. I am grateful for the permission of the British Library to reproduce the two pages of Harleians Ms 6380 shown as photographs before pages 1 and 66 of the book and to Roger Penhallurick at The Royal Institution of Cornwall and Nick Johnson at Cornwall Archaeological Unit, for permission to use their photographs.

x

Finally, my wife, Sonia, has been a constant source of encouragement and help, not only tolerating the inordinate quantity of time and money that this project consumed, but also checking the text several times, making many useful suggestions on presentation, and proof reading each new draft of the book.

I warmly and gratefully acknowledge all of the help I have received and apologise for any unintentional omissions.

INTRODUCTION

I

The Harleian Manuscript 6380 is possibly the most important previously unpublished document relating to the Cornish tin industry. From at least the early eighteenth century the manuscript book has been known as 'The Bailiffe of Blackmore'. The author was the bailiff of the Stannary of Blackmoor, a position of responsibility that required a sound practical knowledge of all aspects of the tin industry. The manuscript book was written in 1586, according to the testimony of the author (pp. 33, 40, 87), and consists of one-hundred and eleven sides or pages, with most pages containing between 35 and 40 lines. There is a religious poem at the beginning of the manuscript, which appears to have been written by a much later hand. It contains three verses thus:

Considerations on 88th Psalm

Heavy O Lord on me Thy judgment lyes
And Curs'd I am; for God neglects my cry.
O Lord in Darkness and Despair I groan
And every Place is Hell, for God is Goode.
O Lord arise and let thy (<u>illegible</u>) control
These horrid clouds that press my frighted soul
O Rise and save me from Eternal Night.
Thou that art the God of Light.

2.

Downward I hasten to my destined Place,
There none obtain thy aid none sing thy Praise,
Soon I shall lye in Deaths deep ocean drowned,
Is mercy there; Is sweet forgiveness ffound,
O save me yet whilst on the Brink island,
Rebuke the storm and set me safe to Land,
O make my longings & thy mercy sure.
Thou that art the God of Pow'r.

3.

Behold the weary'd Prodigal is come,
To thou his Hope; his harbour & his home.
No Father he could find; no friend abroad,
Deprived of Joy and Destitute of God.
O let thy horrors and his anguish and

Be Thou his Father and be thou his Friend,
Forgive the son thou didst so long reprove.
Thou that art the God of Love.

The manuscript has been credited to Thomas Beare from at least the second half of the nineteenth century, and to 'Mr Beare' from the early eighteenth century. G C Boase & W P Courtney's *Bibliotheca Cornubiensis* (1874) says the author was Thomas Beare, and cite JRIC 1865 Appendix p.15. The cited article, however, does not give Mr Beare a Christian name. Thomas Tonkin (1733), William Borlase (1758) and William Pryce (1778) all refer to the author as 'Mr Beare'. Thomas Tonkin, the eighteenth century St Agnes historian, was quoted by William Borlase in his *Natural History of Cornwall* (1758) as referring to the author of the 'Bailiffe of Blackmoor' as: "one Mr Beare (who wrote) in the beginning of Queen Elizabeth's reign." In the Introduction to the 1811 'De Dunstanville' edition of Carew, a letter from Tonkin, dated July 9th 1733, has: "one Mr Beare wrote a book of the customs etc of the stannaries, entitled, the Bailiff of Black-more."

Who was Mr (? Thomas) Beare? There is a lot of information about the author in the book itself. Some of this information gives insight into his character and experience, and some provide hints of his age, background and origins. G R Lewis, in *The Stannaries* (1908), leans on this internal source when he wrote: "Thomas Beare, himself a veteran tinner and stannary official of the sixteenth century ...." On page 101 of the manuscript, Beare refers to his presence at a tin wash at Lostwithiel 36 years before. The context indicates that he was an adult at the time. The event must have been about the year 1550, which would probably place Beare's birth before 1530. However, there is a reference by Beare that indicates that he was even older when the document was written. On pages 8-10 he gives an account of a dispute at Truro which he assigns to the latter days of Henry VIII. He was present at Truro as Bailiff of Blackmoor. Henry VIII died in January 1547, so the incident at Truro took place probably in the years 1545-46. As he already held the post of bailiff, a job that required a certain amount of practical knowledge and experience, it must be assumed that he was at least thirty years of age. This would push the period of his birth back to the years 1510-20, and suggests that he would have been in his 70s when he wrote the book. We must discount Tonkin's and Borlase's dating of the manuscript to the early years of Elizabeth's reign (the 1560s) because of the testimony of Beare himself.

What was Beare's background? There are two Beare (Bere/Beer/Beyre/Beere) families from which he might have sprung. The Beare family of Pengelly in Breock are contenders as are the Beares of Trevedo in Warleggan. The latter family appears on the face of it to have the best claim. Trevedo was a mining district. The name Thomas appears frequently in the Visitation details for the Beares of Trevedo. One Thomas Bere (Beare), who married Sibbell daughter of John Doyngell of Benethwood, lived at the appropriate time and, by the large number of children he fathered, not only survived to a reasonable age but was also apparently quite healthy. One William Doyngell was mentioned on page 11 as representing Foweymoor Stannary at a convocation held at Tavistock in the 14th years of Elizabeth (c.1572). A gentleman called Thomas Bere also attended for Foweymoor.

The writer was a well-read man, seemingly educated above the ordinary. He read Latin and probably French, and his English is well-written, lucid and demonstrates a wide vocabulary. The many colloquialisms he uses were not considered 'slang' in his day. Like William Carnsew, his contemporary, Beare appears familiar with writings of many kinds. He quotes the Bible, Latin and Greek verses, and is familiar with parliamentary records, legal judgements, Cornish and national records, as well as current histories. That he takes issue with popular ideas — for example whether the Jews actually worked the Stannaries, and the extent of their influence — shows an independent mind, more than willing to argue his case against widely-held views. His explanation of the issues involved in the Brokehouse case, his definition of 'who is a tinner', and his grasp of the subtleties of bound ownership, also indicate a sound and astute brain.

Beare had an enquiring mind and a conscientious attitude, so that where difficult or complicated skills needed explaining, in order to ensure that his reader understood what he was trying to say, he endeavoured to learn the basics of those skills himself. He did not claim to be a skilled tin blower, but he did learn the techniques of blowing, including the preparation of the blowing house, in order to explain how the white tin was produced. He was not a skilled tin dresser, but he learned the 'tricks of the trade' in order to be able to pass some understanding on. He was familiar with the measurements and definitions used in Blackmoor Stannary, but he went out of his way to learn about Foweymoor measurements and practices in order to draw comparisons.

Unusual for one of the gentry, Beare held the ordinary tinner in high esteem; respected his skills; admired his virtues; appreciated his humour and regarded his charity toward his fellow tinner as deserving of the highest praise.

Although Beare was born into a lesser gentry family and was tolerably well-educated, probably at least attending a Cornish grammar school, he nevertheless had to work for his living. The detail in his book shows that if he did not actually participate in the menial tasks of digging and dressing the ore, he had worked sufficiently close to these operations to know precisely how the tasks were performed and what constituted good and bad practice. His description in the concluding part of the book shows knowledge of blowing, and although it is apparent that he is not a skilled blower, he takes pride in the fact that he can do the job with a reasonable degree of competence. His knowledge of the tinners' secrets, with respect to checking black tin purity, ensuring correct weights and measurements, as well as noting the tricks the skilled tinners played on the unsuspecting occasional helpers, indicates that Beare had learned his job whilst working among the tinners. His deep knowledge and understanding of their skills, habits, attitudes and customs demonstrate Beare's close observation of his subject.

II

The position of bailiff needs explanation, as do the responsibilities and tasks of the other principal officials in the stannary arrangement. At the head of the Stannary of Cornwall (and Devon) stood the Lord Warden, or Chief Warden, as he was known in the twelfth century, when the earliest reference to him was made. The Lord Warden was always a great magnate and usually a favourite courtier. The job was largely a sinecure, from which the holder of the office received financial benefit, and usually only involved himself in the Stannaries from either court or Westminster. The Lord Warden had a deputy known as the Vice Warden. This position tended to be occupied by a Cornish gentleman of note, who would normally have had an interest in the tin industry. The Vice Warden actually ran the Stannary on behalf of the Lord Warden. The Vice Warden acted for the Lord Warden in all matters, including presiding over the Great Court, where issues involving the whole Stannary were resolved. The jury in the Great Court, which sat only occasionally, was made up of 24 jurors, six being elected from each of the four stannaries. The mayors of the four coinage towns of the four stannaries effectively appointed the six jurors who represented the interests of the tinners in their own stannary.

Below the Vice Warden were four stewards, each representing one of the four stannaries. These stewards had total jurisdiction over their respective stannaries. They presided over the Steward's Courts, which had developed since the thirteenth century to take care of all matters involving the day to day running of the stannaries. These courts were held quite regularly, usually every three weeks, and settled problems of a purely local nature — disputes over bound ownership or water rights were commonest — that did not concern the whole Stannary of Cornwall or Devon. The Steward's Court was itinerant. Its main activity was to register new bounds and renew old ones. Records from the early sixteenth century, for Penwith & Kerrier Stannary, show that over a period of months the Steward's Court met in Goldsithney, Helston, Redruth and Lelant. The steward presided over this regular petty court and he was assisted by jurors. Issues that were not satisfactorily settled by the Steward's Court could be appealed to the Warden's Great Court.

Next in importance to the steward was the bailiff. Each of the four stannary districts had a bailiff who was answerable to the steward. The bailiff was the man who actually supervised the smooth-running of each stannary. He was at the sharp end of the whole stannary administration. His was the task of visiting the hundreds of individual bounds, spread across dozens of moors and bals. He had to become familiar with every water supply, every controversial side bound, every set of stamps, every blowing house and the entire system of security involved in the carriage of white tin to the coinage towns and its safety once there. The silting of fresh-water rivers was his concern, as were adequate forage and grazing for charcoal burners' horses, the correct measurements for charcoal sacks and for weighing black tin and the correct blowing house marks indicating the house, the blower and the quality of the white tin. When a tinner needed arresting, the gaol keeper disciplining, a debt collecting, a writ serving, a petition presenting, violent dispute settling or 'shovell money' collecting, it was the bailiff who had to do it or see that it was done. Failure to perform any of the above tasks laid the bailiff open to arrest or fine himself. He ensured that tinners registered their bounds at the itinerant stannary courts and that their registration was legitimate.

Petty officials working under and answerable to the bailiff were the tollers, porters, peisers, comptrollers and the receivers. The toller appears to have been a sort of assistant bailiff, who stood in or deputised for him when he was sick or otherwise unavailable (footnote page 38). The porters were labourers whose main task was to shift the heavy white tin blocks to the weighing scales, and once weighed and coined (a corner of each block was removed for assay), remove the tin to a secure place prior to shipping out. The peisers job was to check the weight of each tin block. They had charge of the 'Queen's beam' and of the standard Winchester measure for checking the correct weights. The comptrollers had various duties including discipline and security, so that the gaol and the gaol keeper came under his charge. The receivers looked after the accounts. They ensured that every fine, due, toll, tribute and fee was paid and correctly entered in the stannary accounts. All these petty officials were subject to the bailiff and through him to the steward of their stannary.

Information on the above described arrangements can be found in Richard Carew *Survey of Cornwall* (1602), R R Pennington *Stannary Law* (Newton Abbot 1973), G R Lewis *The Stannaries* (Harvard 1908), T Pearce *The Laws & Customs of the Stannaries of Cornwall & Devon* (1725), J Tregoning *The Laws of the Stannaries of Cornwall* (1808), *The Laws of the Stannaries of Cornwall* (1753) and in the text of *The Bailiff of Blackmoor*. The positions, duties, organisational arrangements and definitions all changed and developed over several centuries, and so the above was true at times to some extent, but probably never precisely as described at any particular time.

III

The contents of the book are given on pages 91-94 and 111. The 'chapter' headings given in the tables of contents are not worded in precisely the same way as at the heads of those 'chapters'. There are also some headings missing in the tables. The page numbers are, likewise, not always the same as in the text. For example, the table of contents on page 91 gives: 'Duties chargeable in the Awdite for Blackmoor stannary. p.4.' On page 4 the heading is: 'Thes are the particulars that the bayliffe shalbe charged with all uppon his accompt yerely payable upon the xith or xiith day of Octobre.' These headings mean the same although having differing detail. The heading on page 6: 'What be they that ar tinners.' is not found in the table of contents. The table of contents on page 93 (line 24) gives: 'Off wages of Tynners & of their estate. (page) 53.' This heading, although differently worded, is actually found on page 56. Thus, although the contents of the book can reasonably be established by reference to these tables, care must be exercised when using them.

The author has several topics he wishes to explain or argue. He sets out to explain the history of the stannaries, with special emphasis upon the important part that the gentlemen of Blackmore played. To this end he studied the historical background of the thirteenth and fourteenth century Crown involvement in the operation of the stannaries. Who actually ran them? How did the stannary arrangement get started in the form that it did? What did the Royal Charters state? How were the arrangements modified at the end of Edward III's reign? These were the sort of questions Beare sets out to answer.

Beare also sought to explain the many legal devices involved in running the stannary system. He does this by explanation and example. His examples tend to be cases, originally in Latin, but which we have rendered into English, that best illustrate the point he is making. For example: On page 31 he explains how tinbounds were registered and then gives an actual registration. On page 46, after explaining how *distringas* works he gives 'The forme of a *Distrangas*' in Latin. This is followed by similar Latin examples of 'The forme of the Warrant' and 'The forme of the write(writ) of *fieri facias.*'

Some of the most interesting parts of the book are those that deal with the tinners themselves. Their customs, humour, economic setup, diet, charity and their view of outsiders, are all described with sympathy, delicacy and understanding. Beare is never patronising about the tinners. His admiration for their toughness, independence, courage in adversity and kindness toward each other, especially toward the sick or those poorer then themselves, is quite genuine.

IV

The background to Beare's book is one of change in an industry and county where things had remained relatively constant for centuries. Cornwall and the tin industry were affected by the many technological, economic, social and governmental changes in England during the sixteenth century. Government control of the regions was becoming more centralised and European influence was being felt in all English institutions.

In many ways the basic organisation of the stannaries and the fundamental relationships between wealthy landowners (and mineral lords), London merchants, small self-employed tinners and the increasing number of wage earners, remained similar to what they had been when the Tudors first came to the English throne. However, the speed of economic and technological change had accelerated and the tinners felt these changes in their industry to a more noticeable degree than had their forefathers. Sixteenth century wage and commodity price inflation affected Cornish tinners no less than the rest of the country's population. Rent increases, new poor law provisions, central government interference, growing population and pressure on crop-growing land, all served to add to the problems of tinners in sixteenth century Cornwall.

Added to this general background of change and occasional crisis was a fundamental shift in the way that the tin industry operated. Throughout the Medieval period, tin-working meant mostly streaming the moors for alluvial tin, and, to a lesser degree, searching for 'shode' or eluvial deposits. Digging into the outcrop of mineralised structures (lodes/veins) for the tin ore, although undoubtedly an ancient practice, was not a usual or common method until well into the fifteenth century. Whilst rich, alluvial beds were still available there was no pressing need to dig into the hard rock for lode tin. As alluvial streaming gradually produced less tin, the tendency to seek out the source lodes increased.

By the middle of the fifteenth century lode mining, by means of openworks (trenching), or by shafts and levels, was becoming widespread. Early sixteenth century bound records show that lode workings were rapidly overtaking streamworks in importance, especially in the western stannaries. By the time of Thomas Beare, the western districts of Penwith, Kerrier and Tywarnhayle, were dominated by lode workings, although in Foweymore and Blackmore streaming remained the more common method of winning tin. Important examples of lode workings, as at Mulberry, Colliford and Trevedo, indicate that even in the east the shift was away from streaming, although its successful pursuit continued right through to the twentieth century.

Beare's account of the industry's history from the thirteenth century till his day, together with his description of how the stannaries functioned in the 1580s, is all the more interesting and significant because of this background of change in which he wrote it. Showing through everything he wrote is the feeling of his awareness that the old order, still very much in evidence, was being replaced. Continuity and change were manifest in every aspect of life for the tinners and their ancient industry.

V

In order to facilitate ease of comparison and checking of the text by users of this transcription, the line and page layout of the original Harleian MS 6380 has been kept. Where we believe that a marginal gloss was intended by the author for inclusion in the text it has been inserted in the appropriate place. Marginal comments are referred to in <u>Notes & Comments</u>, under the page number.

Abbreviated words have been rendered in full, thus 'wth' and 'wt', 'wch', 'pt', 'pfytt', 'y̧', 'y̧' and 'y̧' are rendered with, which, part, profytt, that, the and them. Beare frequently used the Old English 'thorn' in the shape of a 'y', which is equivalent to the modern 'th'. In each case it has been rendered as 'th' for clarity and consistency. Generally, throughout, words have been given Beare's original spelling. There is very little punctuation in the text and this has been left unaltered. Occasionally, capital letters have been given to proper nouns where none were originally there. Where Latin has been translated, punctuation has occasionally been added.

Most of the Latin text quoted by Beare has been translated by Robert Petrie, of the Cornwall Record Office. His efforts have been hampered by my imperfect transcription of the original Latin of Beare. I have compared and occasionally either corrected or supplemented my transcription with the same texts as rendered by others. Thomas Pearce and G R Lewis's books have been used for this purpose.

VI

The tables of contents appear at the end of the book in the original (on pages 91-94 and page 111), however, it is appropriate to reproduce them at the beginning also. The headings vary between the text and the tables and some of them are not too clear, thus they have been paraphrased.

VII

Thomas Beare's book is undoubtedly a classic, not for its literary style or beauty of language, but due to the sheer breadth of its content, and the deep understanding of the subject displayed by the author. Beare missed few areas of the tin industry in his study. Late twentieth century Cornish miners, whether their experience is of Wheal Jane, Wheal Pendarves, Wheal Concord, Mount Wellington, Wheal Maid, Geevor or of South Crofty, still soldiering on toward the twenty-first century, will recognise much in this book. So many attitudes and characteristics of sixteenth century tinners remain among the miners of South Crofty, many of whom have moved to the mine as theirs have closed. This continuity and sense of place in the historical development of an industry which dates from centuries before Christ, is an unusual if not unique part of the nature of Cornish miners. It is to be hoped, that not only mining researchers, but the miners themselves, will enjoy reading and benefit from this transcription of Thomas Beare's wonderful book.

Off the working in Tinworkes by the Saxons
whereby tinners call Jewes working.

It appeareth by working of our Tinners in Cornwall that the Saxons being heathen people (when
they inhabited our country) were skillfull workers of and search for black tyn, with in
those auncient dayes wrought not with spades
working tooles made with Iron as we have now
in our tyme but all of the hart of oake. they
at they got their tyn had their blowing houses
and places hard by their workes, no it maketh
whole, for proof wherof of divers workers of
our tyme have found their shovells spades &
mattox made all of oke ye holme in divers and
sundry places at they have digged be tyme
in old waste ground. they have found white
tin blowen likewise already in the places no
doubt but they have removed for the most
vpon mynerall good working and have had
great wealth. But what Beborough were either
Saxons or Danes or any other nations, our tyn
workers & Gvaliardes call and terme their
places by the name of the working of Jewes
with I cannot by any wa in iudge to be trew.
for although it is most manifest that there were
Jewes inhabiting here with in our realme vntill
the yeere of our lord god 1291. I neuer heard
nor reade that they had libertie to seek & worke
for tyn. because they had alway their dwellings
in great townes and citties. And being great
vsurers were in the yere banished out of England
amounting to the number of fifteene thousand
and therefore sent by the noble prince king
Edward the first in the twentith yeere of his
raygne. after with time they were neuer permitted to dwell in the realme of I cheu-well of
them by continuance of tyme. the tynners had
tyme great ghests to their tyn, wrought from
tyme to tyme by custome vntill the reigne

Off the working Tinworkes by the Saxons
which tinners call Jewes working.
It appeereth by working of our Tinners in Corn=
wall that the Saxons being heathen people(when
5   they inhabited our Country) were skillfull wor=
kers of and sercers for black tyn, which in
thos auncient dayes wrought not with spades &
working tooles made of Iron as we have now
in our tyme but all of the hart of oake, they
10   as they got their tyn and their blowing houses
and places hard by their works and so made it
white, for prooff where of diverse workers of
our tyme have fownd their shovells spades &
mattox made all of oke & holme in divers and
15   sundry places as they have serched for tinne
in old waste grownd they have fownd white
tin blowen likewise already in which places no
doubt but they have chanced for the most part
upon principall good working and have had
20   great wages. But what so ever they were either
Saxons or Danes or any other nations our tin
workers & Spaliards call and terme their
places by the name of the working of Jewes
which I cannot by any reason judge to be trew
25   for although it is most manifest that there were
Jewes inhabiting heer within our Realme untill
the yeer of our lord god. 1291. I never heard
nor read that they had libertie to seek & worke
for tyn because they had always their dwellings
30   in great towns and cities. And being great
usurers were in that yeere banished out of England
amounting to the number of fifteene thowsand
and three score persons by the noble prince king
Edward the first in the twentith yeer of his
35   Raigne, after which time they were never per=
mitted to dwell in the Realme that I ever read of
thus by continuance of tyme, the tynners ha=
ving great profyts by their tyn, wrought from
tyme to tyme by custome untill the xxxiij th
yeer

yeer of the Raigne of King Edward the first
being in the yeer of our Lord God 1305. then
was it thought good to the tynners to procure by
Charter from the prince freely to graunt unto them
5   libertie to dig and serch for tin in any place where
tyn might be fownd and a court to determine
all matters and causes betwene tynner and
tynner which prerogative of a Court could not
be obtened without a Corporacion that is to weet free=
10   holders which must bynd their heires by theire
inheritance to aunswere to the said Court where
upon the inhabitants of this stannary of Black=
moor having great care to bring this sute to good
effect; for & in the name of the whole
15   Sheere obtayned the said grant of and from the
prince of famous memory King Edward the first
as by the said Charter to the tynners grantid
hereafter contayned more plainely it doth and
may appeer and is now called by the name of
20   one stannary only although devided into fower
severall stannaryes for ease of the whole body
of the Sheer. In thos dayes there were certaine
gentlemen dwelling within this stannary of Bla=
ckmoore cheifly in thees parishes. St Austell
25   Luxulian Lanlivery Roche Ewa St Stephen
in Brannell, St Mewham and St Dennis
which offered to bind their landes & their heires
for evermore to answere to the Court of the
said Stannary of Blackmore the names of
30   which gentlemen ar as folow Prideaux La=
veddon Heale, Tomyow, Lestowen, Bescowen & Renould
tinners. theis gents I say not only binding them selfes
& their heires within the said severall parishes to answere at
every law court within the said Stannary, ar unto
35   this tyme amerced if they appeer not at the court
But also there were within the precinct of the said
parishes amongst others eight gentlemen which bownd
their tithinges
wholy to appeer and to do sute to the said court at
every

Every law day which as well have entrid their
fines then presently yeerly to be paid for ever as
also eight tithing men to serve the court conti=
ually, to weet one tithing man for every of the
5 said tithings which have continued unto this pre=
sent day in their full force whose names &
fines hereafter ensue that is to weet

Decemnar de Trethewye	ijs
Decemnar de Boswthgye	vijs
10 Decemnar de Treverbin	vjs
Decemnar de Predis	ijs
Decemnar de Trenance Austell	ijs iiijd
Decemnar de Tremodres	viijs
Decemnar de Tregorreck	vjs
15 Decemnar de Demilliack | vs |

Sum xxxviijs.ivd. *

Besides all theis there be other tithins which pay a yerly
fine to their prince and are not bownd to do any sute
at all to the said court which dutie is yeerly receavid
20 collected and paid into thexchequer by the bayliffe of
the said stannary which amounteth to the sum of three
pownd and od mony whereof a great part by meanes
of antiquitie of the time is lost, so far forth that the
bayliffes of this time knoweth not wher to seek
25 much of the particulars of it, howbeit he shalbe com=
pelled to levy the whole to the Audit you shall under=
stand that the place appointed for the principall corts
aforsaid to be kept in old time is unto this day called
Hallew alias Haledew being a Cornishe name & is
30 as much to say in the Englishe tongue Blackmoore
then is there another dutie likewise yerely paid
into the Quenes Exchequer of the said stannary
of Blackmoor called Tribulage alias shovellmony
this dutic is only collected and gathered of all tin=
35 ners working & serching for tin within the hundred
of Pyder of every tinner working within the said
hundred yeerly that is or ought to be collectid
one halfepenny for this collection the baylife
payeth into thexchequer yerely of a certaintie
40   vijs.viijd.

Lead Seal of the 1305 Stannary Charter. The Seal was re-discovered in 1842 near Bath. The Latin
inscription translates: ''The Seal of the Community of Cornish Tinners.''

Thes are the particulars that the bayliffe
shalbe charged with all uppon his ac=
compt yerely payable upon the xjth
or xijth day of Octobre.

5 *De fine liberoru' tenciu'*
   De Extrahur'
   De certo Dono ..... xxxviijs. iiijd.
   De fine stann' ..... iijli.
   Aliis p'quisit Cur'

10 All theis have I set downe here for none other
    cause but that it may appeer most manifestly to the
    reader that as the inhabitants of Blackmoor were
    the only purchasers of the Grant or Charter
    of all the tinners of Cornewall so ar they yeerly
15 burdened with the payment of theis yeerly sums
    And as for the stannaries of ffoymoor Penwith
    Kerrier and Triwarnhaile are charged with no
    more payments but only with the prerequisits and
    amerciaments of their severall Courts. So
20 this Charter being grauntid by the prince and
    delivered to the tinners of Blackmoore & a Comon
    Seale likewise made for the same purpose of a
    pretie bredth having the print in it of one
    working with a spade in a tinwork and another with
25 a picke delivered to them together with the said Charter
    theis the tynners receaving appointid to be kept in the
    tower of Luxullian in a Coffer with eight lockes
    and eight keyes whereof every of the said tithins
    ought to have his key. The Comon Seale of
30 Tinners serveth for this purpose cheifely, that if
    they should be molestid greivid or wrongfully
    troubled contrary to their auncient Customes
    & liberties. They by preferring to the prince or
    to the honorable Counsaill of a supplication of
35 their Comon greifes having their Comon Seale
    thereunto annexed might have the better credit
    at the hands of the most honorable Counsell,
    as now of late dayes yt chaunced the tinners of
    the Duchie of Cornwall and also of Devon to
40 have great occasion ministred unto them in the
    tyme of the Raigne of King Edward the Syxt
                    of

Off famous memory brother to the Queenes
highness now. the trouble fell out after this sort
there is in the Charter of tinners amongst other grants
their wordes expressed   *Et Concessimus p' nobis et*
5 *heredibus n'ris quod omnes stannatores predict'*
totu' stannu' suu' sic ponderatu' licite vendere cuicu'
voluerint in villis predictis faciend inde nobis et
heredibus n'ris Coignagiu et alias consuetudines
debitas et usitatus nisi nos vel heredes nostri
10 *stannu' illud emere volverimus* which being En=
glished containe theis words. We have grantid
also for us and our heires that all our tinners afore=
said all their tyn so weighed lawfully may sell to
whom they will in the townes aforesaid doing thereof
15 to us and our heires the Coynage and other the
Customes due and used. Except we or our heires
will buy the said Tyn our selves. Theis words
of the Charter in forme aforesaid being understand
& espied out by one Gilbert Brokehouse a stranger
20 borne & the great advantage that might ensue thereof
likewise considered. the said Gilbert for a great
sum of mony and with no small sute obtayned &
had out a lease by the dimission and graunt of the
said noble prince. King Edward the Sixt of for & con=
25 cerning the princes prerogative of the sale of all the
whole tyn aswell of Devon as Cornwall for & during
certaine yeres, which Lease being so obtayned, the
said Gilbert joined to him one Thomas Roydon and
coming downe to the Quoynage making a brag
30 that he had brought great treasures couched in lethern
bags upon horses, but (as it was reportid) being
serched nothing els but broad plates of lead
brought it so to passe that no man could be Master of his
owne tyn, for Brokehouse only appointed both sale
35 and price thereof, And when it was alleaged
the tin merchaunts must need have mony presently to
maintaine further poor tinners, the said Brokehouse
made answere that they must abide his leasure. this
the Londoners and thother marchants of whit tyn
40 being

Stept from the market, the marchants of the
black tyn had no mony neither to pay the Coliers for
ther cole neither yet to maintaine forth the spaliards
and laborers in their workes in so much they esteemed
5   them selves utterly undone. to hear the lamentacons
of the poor yt would have mollified a stony hart
this misery of the poor spaliards continued forth
untill the Raigne of Queene Mary in whose raigne
the tynners made sute by their generall supplica=
10   cion sealed with the said Comon Seale of tinners
to have this lease of Brokehouse so called
in question that yt might be made frustrate considering the great
inconvenience that fell out thereby. this matter betwene
the tynners of Devon and Cornwall and the said
15   Brokhouse was ernestly debatid at the Quenes Pa=
lace of Westminster in the xviiith day of Decembre in
the first yeer of Queen Maryes Raigne before
the Lord Chanceler being then Steven Bishop of
Whinchester the Errle of Penbroke, the Bishop
20   of Rochester, the Lord of Bedford the Lord Hastings
the Duke of Northfolke Ser John Gage Ser William
Peter, Sir John Borne and the Lord of Sussex
and at last made utterly frustrate and void
as by the Copie of the decree set out in this book
25   more playnly yt may to the reader appeer.

What be they that ar tinners.

Dyvers men (as saith the poyet) ar of divers opi=
nions *pectoribus mores tot sunt quot in ob ta figurae*
So that hard it were for me to define what is he that is
30   a tinner and cheifely wher as there ar so many of ex=
cellent witts and fine judgements that wil not only con=
troll my simple and rude doings but also bear a
malicious mind towards me to utter that by my pen
which I secretly think in my mind. Some say that men de=
35   serveth not the name of a tinner except he be able
to make his work, get his tyn, washe yt purifie it
and also make his hearth, blow his tinne, & make it white
but if that saying should be true then should ther be
fownd few tynners, or no tynners at all: for

They ar severall mens occupacions and every
of theis qualities maketh a tinner. I have heard
so many reason of the definition of the name of
a tinner & so contrary one to another that I know not
5   what I may say herein. for some their ar being dea=
lers with tyn and so bent to their owne affection
that when occasion of trouble cometh only upon the
tinners other touching their princes service or els
the payment of mony or otherwise. then they say
10   that they are no tynners, on the other part the same
men going about to recover their debts at the hands
of their Creditors and barred thereof by meanes
of a foriners plea set into the Court a=
gainst them then confesse they them selves to be
15   tinners and wilnot stick to implead the same in court
for recovery of their debts, by the stannary court.
Some say the laborers workers & spaliards ar the
tinners, for there is a tinner, a laborer & a worker
for tynne & a spaliar. I take the tinner to be him
20   that geveth wages by the yeer to another to work
his right in a tinwork for him as a dole, or a
halfdole more or lesse or els worketh his
right himselfe as many do, the worker is he that
taketh upon him to sue the tinners right
25   ffor wages by the yeere, or els for lesse tyme the spa=
liar is he that cometh jornies now and then to the
tinworke for his hire and for the day saveth the
worker from spale as tinners terme it: and so by
that occasion is called a spaliar. Surely I think that
30   none repine against me this far forth but that
all theis ar tinners. Now to come to the marchant
that setteth his mony upon black tin and maketh
yt white, having his blowing howse, his stamping
house his Crasing mill, no man can denay but
this man is a master tinner

Amongst theis tynners there ariseth one question as I
myself often times heard. A tynner having right
in a tinwork. A tynner worker for a yere or
two, A Spaliar working for a day or two, the tinner
5   selleth away the right of his tinwork, the worker &
spaliar geveth over their working, all these I saw casting
off their accustomed exercises will now aleage
& say they were tinners in deed but now they are
none, as who saith the smith, the taylor the fuller the
10   weaver, the Carpenter geving over their occupa=
tions ar then no longer Smithes taylors weavers
fullers or Carpenters, whereas in very deed, as I
suppose, A man being once knowen as an ar=
tificer, is alwais accomptid for an artificer, once
15   a tinner & alwais after a tinner. Now let us come
to the marchant that byeth white tyn, as march=
ants of our Country, the Londoner & likewise all
other marchants whatsoerver: theis undoubtidly
when fortune frowneth against the poor tinner
20   will stoutly affirme themselves to be no tinners.
And yet I cannot see by any reason but thes should
be the most principallest tinners of all other for
when they implead forenners to recover their
debts they wilbe tinners and crave the privilege
25   thereof, likewise if question fall out about the bying
of their white tyn, at the Coynage, then to serv
their turn they claime the benefit of the charter
of tinners as I my self can say somewhat of trou=
ble that chanced at the Coynage kept at Truro by my
30   tyme which, (I doubt not) but that there ar diverse
others that can affirm to be true as well as I. it for=
tuned at a coynage kept at Truro in the latter
dayes of the noble prince King Henry the eight father
to our Quenes majestie now that one Hugh Boska=
35   wen a wise man & lerned in the lawes of the Realm
had at that present Coynage a fair bill of tin and
Amongst

Amongst diverse suters that came to him to have
his tyn, one there was being a most principall
suter unto him called ffarneby this man offred
to take his tin at such a high price that his offer
5 was very well liked of with Mr Boskawen, but
on the other part considering that his request was
to have dayes of payment for the mony with this
gentleman waighed nothing at all: for he might
well abide long dayes of payment
10 being a gentleman of great welth. but not
liking the insufficiencie of the man he deman=
ded of ffarneby what sureties he could bring for
the payment of the mony at the dayes by himself
prescribed. ffarnaby at that present tyme having
15 gests repayring to his house and emongst other
there hosted with him a worshipfull knight called
Sir John Arundell of Trerise made answere that he
would bring the said man of worship to be his
suretie, I desire no better suretie quoth Mr Bos=
20 kawen take here this bill of tin said he shew
him to Mr Arundell & bring from him a letter
of his owne hand to pay me at thy dayes appoin=
ted this is as much as I request the said ffarne=
by receaving the bill of tyn at the hands of
25 Mr Boskawne never shewed the same to Mr Arundell
neither yet so much as requestid him to have
his letter or yet to geve his word but went
straight waies to John Caplin marchant dwelling
at Hampton & at that time using the office of re=
30 ceavership of Cornwall and sold the said tin un=
to him verefying his sale to be good by delivering
up the bill likewise to Mr Caplin within a litle
space after that yt chanced that tydings came to Mr
Boskawne that his tyn being at Truro in the
35 Coynage house was brought out of the Quenes
house

Ready to be caried away, which newes much misli=
king him, he posted straightway from his house
to Truro, & procured an officer to arest the said tin
laying greatly to his charge that he had no right or
5   auctoritie to sell away his tin untill suchtime
as he had brought Sir John Arrundles letter for
satisfaction of the mony appointed to be paid at his
owne dayes Mr Caplin being present affirmed that he
had lawfully bought the tin & would surely have it
10   Mr Boskawne said that he should have no tyn of his
ffarnaby being accused by Mr Boskawne & anima=
tid by Mr Caplin confessed his error, that he was
much blame worthy that he brought not Mr Arrundels
letter to Mr Boskawne according to promise, but
15   for amends thereof offered to enter him selfe into
any sum by his owne bond for the true satisfact=
tion of the payments of the said monyes accor=
ding to the said dayes prescribed, but this could
not satisfye Mr Boskawnes mind for that he knew
20   the said ffarneby to be insufficient upon his owne
bond so no remedy was there but this matter of
controversie betwene Mr Boskawne and the tinners
which sticked with him being plentiffes & Mr Caplin &
the marchants which sticked with him of the other party
25   as defendants must needs fall out by tryall of
xxiiij tie of the chevest Customers of tinners
impanneled within the stannary of Blackmoore
as the body of the stannary of the Duchy of Cor=
nwall and a Court sommoned to be kept for
30   Blackmoore at which tyme the writer hereof
being bayliffe brought in his panell at the said
Court kept at Truro before Sir William Godolphin
knight underwarden & cheife steward & William
Beare his under steward, at last hit was

Assentid of both sides that the one half of the
panell should be tinners & thother half marchants
for the better indifferency and equitie of the cause
they being impaneled the witnesses & allegacons being heard and were
5   tryed & sworne their counsells debatid at large in fine that passed
with Mr Caplin & the marchants by reason of the bill
of tyn delivered unto him so that the bill is the only
discharge of the byer. Thus much have I set
forth in writing for that it should manifestly appeer
10   that the marchant byers of tin & clayming to have
redresse of their causes in matters of controversie
concerning the buying of tyn at the Coynage by
the charter of tinners only, ar tynners & so in myne
opinion ar that stewards, customers, Controllers pay=
15   sers & all other officers of the stannary the Conags
and the Courts thereof: In so much that I find no
more diversitie betwene the one and the other
but that the inferior Company of tinners must
needs confesse them selves to be so And that superior
20   Company being rulers at libertie and at the full
election that when they list they ar tynners &
when they list then they ar foreners.

How the Tinners did before the
Charter was grauntid.

25   Now forasmuch as I have said somewhat concerning
the serching for tin before the yeer of our lord
God 1291 and from thensforthe of the purchasing
of the Charter by the tinners of Blackmoore
with the Courts & particular charges thereof issu=
30   ing out yeerly to the prince there resteth now
somewhat to write partly by ancient records fownd
out of their Customs which the tinners had before
the Charter with the Courts & particuler charges
thereof going out yeerly to the prince, there
35   resteth now somewhat to write by auncient re=
cords

partly fownd out of the Customes that tynners had
before the Charter to them grantid. I find that
they alwaies used to work & seek for tyn in
wastrell ground, and also in the princes sev=
5   ralls whereas any tyn might be gotten or had
using likewise lawfull wayes to cary & recary
their tyn to places convenient & necessary to be
dressed clensed and purified. like maner of wise to con=
vey the courses of water to their severall works
10   for the purifying of their tyn. having liberti
likewise to dig mine serche make shafts pitche
bownds & for tyn to worke in places for their
most advantages (excepting only & reserving all
sanctuary grownd churchyeards mils bakehowses
15   and gardens paying & yelding only to the prince
or lord of the soyle the fiftenth foot or boll to
and for the toll of their tyn to farm. provided
alwaies that if it be chansed the said tinners in their
mining to subvert or work up any mans house, or
20   els any highway whereby yt might fall out to
travelers to be troubled in their jornies, then
in this case the tynner or tynners subverting
the premises should to their charge & expences
make or cawse to be made the said howse or high
25   faring way so subvertid & undermined so law=
full and sufficient as they were before the tyme
of their working or undermining all this ye may
perceive by one record of an action of trespas
commenced against one Richard David of Cran=
30   borne a tinner by one John Jenkin and the
answere thereof made by the Counsell of the
said defendant prosequutid in the xxv th yeere
of the Raign of King Henry 8 whose records I
have hereafter writen at large and are as
35   followeth

A plea framed up against a tinner
working in the princes severall grownd
in the yeer of King Henry the eight
with the answere of the same.

5   Richard Davy lately of Camborne in the county of Cornwall
husbandman hasbeen distrained to reply to John Jenkyn
for a plea Because by force and arms he broke a close of
the same John
at Chevender and dug there in the buried soil
and turned over and threw up and over threw his land there
10   through which the same John has lost the benefit of his soil
aforesaid for
a long time and they present his hedges there recently
erected and other things etc to his loss etc and against etc
And wherefore the same John through L.B. his attorney complains
that since the aforesaid Richard Davy on 20th October
15   in the year of the reign of the Lord King now etc the 31st by force and
arms etc broke the close of the same John at Chevender
aforesaid and in this his buried soil, viz 10 acres
of land there has dug and has turned over and thrown over his land, viz
16 acres of land there through which the same John
20   has lost the benefit of his soil aforesaid for a long time viz for
the space of one-and-half years and presents his hedges
viz 20 perches of hedges erected there
And other things etc for his loss 40 and against etc And
therefore he brought forth this suit And the aforesaid Richard
through J.B. his attorney
25   came and defended the action and injury when etc
And he says how far he came by force and arms for which he himself
is in no way
therefore responsible And for this he places himself upon the country
etc. And the aforesaid John likewise and
how far the remainder of the alleged trespass aforesaid
30   is as above the same Richard says that the aforesaid
John ought not to have the aforesaid action against him
Because he says that the aforesaid close and also that
the place is which allegedly
the trespass aforesaid took place

Line 5 onward translated from Latin.

both are and at the aforesaid time at which etc were
the six acres of land with appurtenances at Chivender aforesaid
a parcel of the manor of Tywarnhaile which certain
manor belonged to the most illustrious Edward now prince
5 of Wales And at the time of the aforesaid trespass
was seised in his demesne and has and had
each in fee and no time existed when
the memory of men is contrary he has
such customs within the aforesaid manor that
10 are allowed to all leige men of the lord king
whatever steps or conditions there are
for pitching bounding or making each and every
tin works in whatever place within the manor aforesaid
in which it may be possible to find tin in anywhich place
15 holy or sacred, mill, fishery or garden
whatsoever with existing appurtenances within the aforesaid manor
with the only exception of rendering and at all
times paying therefore to the lord of the manor for the time
being one-fifteenth part of tin therein
20 found on his toll and furthermore to make
and limit with bounds measured and limited from
both parts from head to foot
for their claim such a quantity of the same land of
and for whatever tin works as he might want
25 and also to have ways and paths to come,
go, carry and carry back to and from whatever
of those tin works on and above those lands
within the aforesaid manor just as
seems better to them and to expedite more oppurtunely
30 and to conduct, reduce and divert
water and water courses where and
how often there is work at whatever tin works
on and above whatever lands within
the manor aforesaid just as seems better to them
35 And furthermore the same Richard Davy says
that such use was allowed through the whole time aforeaid

This page translated from Latin.

that any such person in whatever such work or any
such works of tin in form aforesaid
thus by him or by them pitched made limited
and bounded within the manor aforesaid in the
5   same tinwork or tinworks may
freely enter and look for tin there
by digging and having found tin in the same (15th part of that same
tin to the said lord of the manor aforesaid for his toll excepted)
may take and perise without contradiction
10   by disturbance or vexation by anyone unless
if he wishes to work and dig in any house or path
to look for tin he aught to preserve
the house and not damage the path that then he
must rebuild the house and that path and either or both of them
15   sufficiently and as good as new just
as the house and that way aught to be or if 100 such
princes of that servant owned it. And furthermore the same
Richard Davy says for himself that the aforesaid 6 acres
are and at the aforesaid time which etc were
20   a parcel of the manor aforesaid and stannary the same
Richard at the time at which etc broke the aforesaid close
in the aforesaid six acres of land and he made therein pitches
and pits in the tin works with bounds measured
and limited from both parts from head to foot
25   in form aforesaid in order
to look for tin in the same by digging in the soil
and he tilled and threw over the earth just as
he is well allowed to do. Which certain breaking of the close
digging of the land, tilling and turning over of the aforesaid land

This page translated from Latin.

In the aforesaid 6 acres of land is the reason for
that same trespass which the said John Jenkin
seeks from him and he is prepared to verify this far which he seeks
judgement if the aforesaid John Jenkin must have his action aforesaid
5   against him.

That the Customers of the stannary
may be charged by the steward at the law
day concerning any custom herein contayned.

Although I have herein already declared & mean
10 here after more at large to declare my simple
knoledge touching the Customes of this stannary of
Blackmoor in this present book yet wil I not
affirme that all things herein contayned ar the very
Custome in deed, for *Consuetudo est a tempore cuius*
15 *memoria hominu' non ixistit in Contrariu'*. A
Custome is from such tyme as any man cannot
remember the contrary. Surely I am throughly
persuaded in this that there ar diverse being both wise
and well learned that can say very largely & pithely
20 touching the Customes of tynners yf they list
whose help I would not stick most humbly to
crave if I might any thing learne at there
hands, or els know them out from the rest.
therefore this much I alleage for my self that to
25 my knowledge I have writen nor here after in=
tend to write nothing here but such usages as I
being charged upon myne othe dare with a safe
conscience to justifie to be Customes as far as ever
I could know meaning farther to omit no alle=
30 gations that touchethe the Customes of the stanary
as far forth as I can call them to my remembrance
In reciting whereof I wholy submit my selfe
&, Correction of thes questions herein con=
tayned to the judgement of Customers of Blackmoore at
35 any law Court to be holden for the said stanna=
ry. All which, law court yf they happen to fynd any
thing herein mencioned to be no Custome at all
which is here recited to be a Custome, yet the
wryting of them in these books ought not to be
ill thought of

Lines 1-5 translated from Latin.
Lines 14,15. Latin translation found in lines 15-17.

ffor yt bringeth the Steward in remembrance
to learne the Custome of them, upon your othes
concerning a doubtfull question which otherwise
happely might never be thought upon. As I
5   have knowen often tymes that when the steward hath
bin doubtfull concerning a question fallen out
betwene party and party the meaning to be resolved
therein hath oft tymes charged the Jury upon
their othes to resolve him in that behalfe and to
10   bring in their Veredict. Now as concerninge
the troubell betwene the tynners of Cornwall &
Devon of the one part and Gilbert Brokehouse
a stranger borne of the other part, whereof is
mention made before (iii pagina) I have annexed hereafter
15   next following the true Copie of the decree
word for word which was grantid in the first yere
of the Raigne of Quene Mary.

        The Coppie of the decree of the Coun=
        sell betwene the tynners of Devon &
20   Cornwall of the one party and Gilbert
        Brokehouse of the other party.

In the matter in variance depending betwene the
Tynners in the Cownty of Cornwall & Devon
in the one party and Gilbert Brokehouse a
25   stranger born of thother party, for & concerning
a Lease made by the excellent prince of famous
memory Edward the syxte unto the said Gilbert
Brokehouse of the date of the xv th of Aprill
last passed for the preferment to the said
30   Gilbart of the buying of tyn to be gotten within
the Cownties aforsaid for certaine yeeres mencio=
ned in the said lease with this condicion expre=
ssed in the said lease that is to say: If that any prejudice
shall hereafter happen or grow unto the said
35   tynners of Cornwall and Devon by or through
the occasion of the said lease contrary to the mea=
ning of theis present Indentures & the same law
               fully proved

Before the most honorable prevy Counsell
of our said Soveraigne lord his heires and
successors. then our said soveraigne lordes
pleasure is and the said Gilbert Brokehouse
5   is also agreed that the said Gilberts interest of and
in the premisses shall from & after such prove
made & warning geven to the said Gilbert Brokhous
or his assignes seal & no farther to be put in ure
as in the said Indenture at large more plainly
10   may appeere: fforasmuch as it hath bin well &
substancially proved before us, that the execution of the
said lease hath bin already prejudiciall to the said
Cownties And if it should continew & take effect
yt shalbe to the hinderance losse & damage of all
15   the Marchants of this Realme & cheefly Mar=
chant tynners & tyn workers of that Contryes
of Cornwall & Devon. We ther fore by the Queen's
highnes comaundment after dew examinacons of thalle=
gacons made in the behalfe of the inhabitants of the
20   the said Cownties Cornwall & Devon and such an=
swere as the said Gilbert Brokhouse made unto the
same and the depositions of certaine witnesses deposed
in that matter well considered Do decree & pronownce the
said lease & demise being condicionall as aforsaid to
25   have fayled in the said Condican in that and for
as much as the use & continuance of the said lease
hath bin as and should be hereafter more and more
hurtfull & prejudiciall to the said Cownties to bee
utterly void frustrate of none effect foresee=
30   ing never the lesse that his decree or anything therein
contayned extend not to impaire or touch the Quenes
highnes prerogative royall annexed unto her highnes
Crowne as her awncesters heretofore have had and
might have had: But that her highnes may use the
35   same to have the preferment of the bying of tyn

When yt shall stand with her highnes pleasure
to use the Comoditie thereof. Datid at the Quenes
highnes palace of Westminster the xviij th of Decembre
in the first yeer of her graces most prosperous
5   Raigne.

Subscribed with the hands of the honora=
ble Counsell whose names follow.

Stephus Winter Cancell	Henry Genegen
Winchester	T.Northfolke
10 Penbrook	John Gage
Robt Rochester	Willm Peeter
Arundell	John Bourne
J.Bedford	Henry Sussex
Edward Hastings	

15   The Coppie of the Charter or first
        Grant confirmed from the tyme of
        King Henry the eight hetherto.

Elizabeth, by the grace of God of England, France and Ireland
Queen, Defender of the Faith, etc. To all to whom these present
20   writings shall come, Greetings. We have inspected these letters
patent of the Lady Mary of blesed memory, lately Queen of England,
our dearest sister, of a confirmation made
in these words: Mary by the grace of God of England, France
and Ireland, Queen, Defender of the Faith, to all to
25   whom these present writings shall come, Greetings. We have inspected
the letters of Lord Edward, lately King of England our
brother (which he) made in these words: Edward VI by the grace of God
of England, France and Ireland, King, Defender of the Faith,
and of the Church of England and Ireland, on earth the Supreme
30   Head to all to whom the present writings
shall come, Greetings. We have inspected the letters patent
of Lord Edward I, lately King of England our ancestor,
made in hese words: Edward, by the grace of God
King of England, Lord of Ireland and Duke of Aquitaine,
35   to the archbishops, bishops, ministers and every
faithful bailiff, Greetings. Know you that for the
                        correction

Line 18 onward translated from Latin.

of our stannaries of the county of Cornwall and for
the tranquility and use of our tinners
of that place have conceded for ourselves and our heirs that
all tinners aforesaid working in those stannaries
5   who are in our demesne whilst they are working in
these same stannaries are free and quit of the pleas
of bondmen and of all pleas and quarrels whatsoever
concerning our court or that of our heirs
that they may not respond there in the presence of any of our judges
10   or ministers or of our heirs for
any plea or quarrel arising within the aforesaid stannary
except in the presence of our warden of our stannaries
aforesaid, who is at that time (for the time being) except pleas
of land and of life and of limb, nor retiring from
15   their works through a summons of any
ministers of ours or of our heirs except through
a summons of our said warden, And that they are quit
of all tallages, tolls, stallages and
aids and other customs whatsoever in the towns,
20   ports, fairs and markets in the aforesaid county for
their own goods, We also have conceded to these same
tinners that they might dig for tin and seek
to find tin anywhere in the lands, moors and wastes
of ours and of any other person in the county aforesaid and
                    (to divert) waters
25   and water courses to the tin workings
aforesaid when and how often there is a working and
to buy a (? grove/gear) to make tin just as the ancients
were accustomed to do without impediments from us
or our heirs, bishops, abbots, priors,
30   earls, barons or any other man and that
our warden aforesaid or his lieutenant may hold
pleas of right of way arising between tinners aforesaid
and also between them and other outsiders

This page translated from Latin.

for all trespasses, quarrels and
contracts made in places in which it is worked
within the stannaries aforesaid similarly arising,
And that the same warden has full power to judge
5   the tinners and other outsiders in any such
pleas and
just as the jurers and (?) in those stannaries
are accustomed to, And if any of the aforesaid tinners
are in any way derelict they must be imprisoned
10   by the aforesaid warden, be arrested and in person
at Lostwithiel and nowhere else be guarded and
detained securely while they deliberate the law and
custom of our kingdom. And if
any of the said tinners against some deed within
15   the county aforesaid not touching the stannary aforesaid
may come to have a jury enquiry, one half
of the jurors for that same enquiry
may be of tinners aforesaid, and the other half
of outsiders. And for a deed totally touching the stannary
20   aforesaid, enquiries may be made just as far as
is usual by custom to be done. And if any of these same
tinners were to be fugitive, or outlaw
or any derelict be made for which his chattels
must be lost, these chattels may be appraised throught he warden
25   aforesaid, and our coroners of the aforesaid county
and through them at the nearest village
kept to answer there to us
and our heirs in the presence of our justices
in eyre in the county aforesaid. We wish furthermore
30   and firmly command that all tin
both white and black wherever it has been found
or worked in the aforesaid county
must be weighed at Lostwithiel, Truro
or Helston by our scales

This page translated from Latin.

for this ordained and signed under the working of all
tin aforesaid, and that all that tin be counted
in those same towns in single measures in the presence of the warden
aforesaid, before St Michael's Day in September under
5   the metal-working aforesaid. And we concede for ourselves and
our heirs that all our tinners can sell all the
aforesaid tin thus correctly weighed
wherever they wish in the towns aforesaid
doing there for us and our heirs coinage
10   and other customs owed and accustomed unless
we or our heirs wish to buy that tin
for which we wish and firmly command
for ourselves and our heirs that our tinners
aforesaid, may have all liberties, free
15   customs and immunities aforesaid,
And that to them without occasion or impediment
of us or our heirs, justices
escheators, sheriffs or other our bailiffs or
ministers whatsoever they may reasonably enjoy
20   and use in form aforesaid. These venerable fathers being witnesses
William of Coventry and Lichfield,
Stephen of Salisbury, John of Carlisle, bishops, Henry
de Lord, Earl of Lincoln, Ralph of Monte,
Henry Earl of Gloucester and Hertford, Humphry
25   de Bohun, Earl of Hertford and Essex, Adam
of Valencia, Hugh de le de Spencer, John
of Hastings and others. Given by our hand at
Westminster 10th day of April in the
33rd year of our reign. We however
30   accept the letters aforesaid, and each and everything in the same
contained, reckoned had and granted by us and
our heirs as far as we are able
and approve and to our beloved tinners
of the aforesaid stannary in the tenor as above we ratify and

This page translated from Latin.

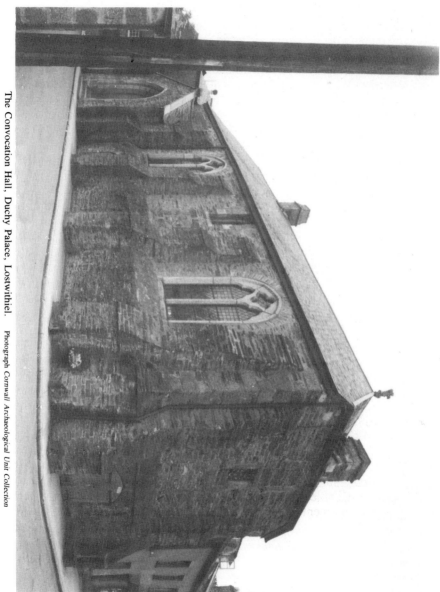

The Convocation Hall, Duchy Palace, Lostwithiel.   Photograph *Cornwall Archaeological Unit Collection*

confirm just as by the aforesaid letters are reasonbly
witnessed, In witness of which thing we have
caused to be made these our letters patent, witness by me at
Westminster 13th day of June in the first year of our reign.
5   We however accept and approve the aforesaid letters
and each and everything in the same contained reckoned
had and granted by us and our heirs
as far as we are able and to
our beloved tinners of the said stannary
10   in tenor aforesaid we ratify and confirm
just as in the aforesaid letters were reasonably witnessed.
In witness of which thing we have caused to be made these our
letters patent. Witnessed by me at
Westminster 30th day of April in the first year of our reign.
15   We however accept and approve the aforesaid letters patent
and each and everything in the same contained reckoned
had and granted by us and our heirs as far as
we are able. And to our
beloved tinners of the aforesaid stannary
20   in tenor aforesaid we ratify and confirm
just as in the aforesaid letters are reasonably witnessed.
In witness of which thing we have caused to be made these
our letters patent. Witnessed by me at
Westminster 10th day of February in
25   first year of our reign.

A true Copie of the Charter or
grant made by King Edward
the first Englished verbatim.

Edward by the grace of God King of England
30   Lord of Ireland and Duke of Aquitaine
to all Archbisshops and Bisshops Abbots
Priors Errles Barons Justices shiriffs
provostes, ministers and to all Bayliffes & other
his faithfull subjects greeting. Know ye that we
35   for the amendment of our stannaryes in the
Cownty of Cornwall and for the quiet & profyt
of our tinners of the same have grantid for us
and our heires that all tinners aforsaid working
in thes stannaries

Lines 1-25 translated from Latin.

which ar our Demeanes so long as they work in
the same stannaryes be free and quite from all
pleas of villaines & from all pleas & plaints
of our Court and of our heires & in what
5   manour soever touching so that they shall not aun=
swere before any of our Justices or ministers or of
our heires for any plea or plaint growing
within our stannaryes aforsaid for the tyme being
(pleas of land, liffe or lym excepted) nor that
10   they depart from their workes by somons of any of
the officers of us or our heires but by the somons
of our said warden. And that they be quite from
all tallages Tolles Stallages Aydes & other
Customes what soever for their owne proper goods
15   in the townes portes faires & markets within
the Cownty aforsaid. We have grauntid also to
the same tynners that they may dig tyn & turves for
melting of tyn everywhere in our lands moores
and wastes & of all other persons what soever in the
20   Cownty aforsaid. And the waters & watercourses
for the workes of the stannaryes aforsaid to turne
where & as often as need shalbe & to buy bushe=
ment for the melting of tyn as of old tyme
hath bin accustomed to be done with out let of us or
25   our heires Bishops Abbots Priors Errles
Barons or other persons what soever. And that
our warden aforsaid or his leiftenant hold
al pleas growing betwene the tyners aforsaid
and also betwene them and other foreners
30   of all trespasses plaints & contracts made in
places wherein they worke within the stannaries afor=
said likewise arising. And that the same warden
have free powre to Justifie the tynners aforsaid
& other foreyners in such pleas & to do justice to
35   the parties as right requireth & as heretofore in
those stannaryes hath bin accustomed. And if
any of the said tynners in any thing shall offend

whereby they ought to be imprisoned that they be
arestid by the warden & in our prison of Lostwi=
thiall & not els where be kept & detayned untill
they be delivered according to the law & custome
5   of our Realme. And if any of the tinners
aforsaid upon any fact within the Cownty afor=
said not touching the foresaid stannaries
shall put himself upon the thenquiry of the
Contry one halfe of the Jurors of such enquest
10 shalbe of the tynners aforsaid and thother half
of forenors. And of fact altogether touching
the stannaryes aforsaid the enquests be made as
heretofore they have bin accustomed. And if any
of the same tynners be fugitive or outlawed
15 or Commit any offence for which he ought to loose
his cattles that the same cattle be apprised by the
warden aforsaid and our Coroner of the said
Cowntie & by them to the next villages delivered
to answere thereof to us and our heires before
20 the Justices of Oyer in the Cownty aforsaid,
furthermore we will and straightly comand
that all tyn as well white as black wheresoever it
shal be fownd and wrought in the Cowntie aforsaid
be wayghed at Lostwithiall Truro & Helston
25 by our wayhtes therto ordayned & marked
under the forfeture of all the Tyn aforsaid.
And that all that tyn be coyned in the same towns
yerely before our said warden before the day
of St Michaell in Septembre under the forfey=
30 ture aforsaid. We have granted also for
us & our heires that all our tynners aforsaid all their
tyn so wayed lawfully may sel to whom they
will in the townes aforsaid. Doing thereof to
us & our heires the Coynage and other the
35 Customs Due and used. Except

Except we or our heires will buy the said tyn
our selves wherefore we will and for us and
our heires straighly comaund that our tyners
aforsaid have all liberties free Customes and
5   quitaunces above writen and that the same without
let or impechement of us or our heires Justi=
ces Excheters Sheriffes or other our Bayliffes
or ministers whatsoever they reasonably enjoy use
in forme aforsaid: Thes being witnesses the worthy
10   fathers W. Bishop of Coventre & Lichfeld
S. Bishop of Sarum & J. Bishop of Carlishe
Henry Lacy Errle of Lincolne, Rauf of
Mount Hermer Errle of Glocester and Hum=
phry of Bohun Errle of Herford And Essex
15   Adomer of Valence Hugh Le de Spencer John
Hastings and others geven by our hand at
Westminster the xth day of Aprill in the xxxiijth
yere of our Raigne.

              The maner of Bownding of
20   theire tyn works.

As the wind purgeth and clenseth the chafe dust
cockels evers & other unprofitable seeds from the
pure graine & corne: even so the water clensithe
& fineth the tyn from Call mundick dare gard
25   and other waste matters & filthines without
which water no tyn can be throughly purified
therefore Tynners alwayes covet to have the com=
moditie of a river as nigh their work as they can
for the tynwork which they call a streamwork other=
30   wise a hatchwork being without water is even as
a windmill without wind. Now happely betwene that
pece of grownd which they have hayned or intend
to haine & the rivers there ar peradventure seven
eight more or lesse diverse tynworkes of the which
35   every severall worke doth greatly covet the Com=
moditie of the water. And every worke may
lawfully fet their water from the river which
                the Tynners

Commonly call the yoa without denyall or contra=
diction the one of the other. But the comoditie of
the water must they crave & fet from the river by
a generall order made amongst tyners which order meane
to set downe set
5   tyme that I have described the order & maner of ther
bownding. They use most comonly to make fower
Corner bownds two at the head of the worke &
two more at the tayle in Cutting & turning up 3.
turfes in every corner and so consequently they
10   make their side bownds and head bownds with 3.
turves at every place one directly against another
keping this order round about their said worke ma=
rishe or peece of ground. then go they to their
yoa or river to fet home their water to serve this
15   work or peece of ground which they have bounded
in making a bye leat likewise under the gras for
the water to run under the grasse or sward for the
water to run in from the yoa to their worke which
(as I said before) must happely passe divers tin=
20   workes before it come to their work. In the
fetting of which water out of the river they shalbe
utterly denyed of the owners of the other workes
except it be by this prescribed order following
that is to weet at the bringing out the water from
25   the yoa toward their by leat so made they must
mak as yt were a cundite with three turves
and one turve set over the said three turffes for
the water to run out of the yoa through the said
Cundite which the tyners comonly call a tuele
30   & may properly descend of this Latine word *tutela* for
that it is a fence & preservacion of all the works
that the water runneth by alongst the by leate
to save them from being vacant. this tuele
may be made with stone as the skillfull tinner
35   knoweth how to make yt. Now in observing that
this order to bring out the water throughe
there tuele & so under sward in their by leate &
from that

Convayed closely to the work. No man can
deny them although they conveigh the water
by xx diverse tynworkes for if they should not
observe this prescribed order, the water runing
5   and flowing abrode at libertie bringing garde
& tayles of workes would make all their workes
vacant for the custome is if tayles run into a
worke the space of one yere & a day & not stopt
out then any other may take that worke as vacant
10   and new bownd him, this order as well in
making their tuele as also renuing their
bownds they must diligently observe & keep
yeerly from traine to traine & bownd to bownd
& most cheifly their corner bonds every yere
15   upon theire very day of bownding how beit some
be of opinion that if they kepe well their corner
bownds it is not greatly materiall for a side
bond two or more. thus with their day of bown=
ding they have a yere & a day to save their work
20   which day of bownding they may prevent if they
list & renue before their day limited. But
then it is to be feared if they break their auncient
day preventing the accustomed time they canot
come to their old day againe but then must
25   keep the same day being prevented which
if they over slip & come to their old day some
say they lose their worke, some say they may
renue their bonds of their workes as often as
they list so that of theis questions you may
30   be resolved by tinners sworne at the law day
for of this freely be ye assured that even as the owners
Do watch and observe diligently to keep their
work & not omitt their appointed day for fear
of losing of their work even so ar there o=
35   thers that apply all their studies to find them
negligent in renuing and so to get their
                    workes from them.

Whereof the experience is dayly seene, They
say also that there is yet another remedy to fet water
from the leat of another mans worke to serve your
worke & not put his worke in danger that is to bear
5   a farme to the worke from whence you fet yt for
the use thereof to your worke.

Good working fownd betwene
two peare of bownds.

If any trouble do fall as often tyme yt chanceth that
10   betwene two peare of bownds there ariseth very
good getting uncertin to which of the two workes this
rich peece of grownd so fownd belongeth to pa=
cifie this controversie they draw a line or cord
from one corner bond to another and by that means
15   they find out which of the two pear of bownds
hath best right to that good peece of grownd but
if the peece of grownd be triangle wise or
with round bonds then they meet from side bond
to side bownd & so by that means is the right tryed
20   out.

Whether if a tinner misse his day
for renuing, amending the fault
after his day, before any other can or
may save his bonds & worke.

25   Some say that if a tinner do not renue his bonds
within a yeer & a day if he afterward finding the
fault himselfe doth renue his old bonds that he
pitched at the begining before any other take
the worke void, this saveth his worke although the
30   day be past but there ar a numbre of the con=
trary opinion that a worke being once lost is alwais
lost. this question may be resolved likewise at
the law day amongth the Customers.

How long the tayles being turned
35   out of a tinworke must abide out.

When a tinworke is bownded the tinner must
be circumspect that he suffer no tayles of any
other tynworke to come into his bownd but
must needs put them out that they con=
40   tinue.

Not there one yeere and a day for if they con=
tinew so long within his haine then are his bownds
and workes utterly lost & any other may pitch
thereupon new bonds: but if the old owner
5 can prove that he turned out the said tayles
running into his haine with one yeer & a day
although the tayles continue out not one houre
he saveth his worke for yf the Custome there
be otherwise diverse by craft might loose their
10 workes for then one man watching to get an=
other mans worke from him may cause
tayles of another worke to run into the work that
he mindeth to make voyd & watching upon the
owner of the worke when he espieth him tur=
15 ning out the said tayles then may he turne
them in again straight way and by that
pollicie get the said worke into his owne
hands.

How long a man may keep his
20 work without delivering toll tyn.

The tynners report this to be their custome that the
first yeer they may keep there worke by bounds
In the second yeere it behoveth them to bestow
some charges upon the peece of ground being
25 under their haine and in the third yeer they
must deliver toll tyn within their said bounds
& so to maintaine forth the said bownds with renu=
ing as before mentioned.

If a man lose his bownds whether
30 he lose his tyn hatch that
he is working in.

If the owner of a peare of bownds lost
his bownds for want of renuing having a
worke or tyn hatch working within his haine
35 the working is sufficient to save the hatch
to his owne Comoditie but the new bownder

May cut a peare of bownds round about
his hatch that he shall work no broder but he
may work in depth as far as he list.

Entring his tinworke bownded
5   into the Court bookes.

The old ancient Custome hath bin tyme out
of mind that after the tynner hath pitched
bonds upon the peece of grownd that he hath
taken vacant yt behoveth him straight way
10 at the next court holden within the stanary
where his worke is, to enter his said
work upon the court bookes to the entent that there
it may be proclaymed by three proclamacions at
three severall stanary courts following calling
15 the said worke as well by his old name as also
by a new name for that yt shalbe manifestly known
by the Court what worke yt was that he hath recove=
red as in one proclamacon for a tinwork within
the stannary of Blackmoore for formes sake
20 here after setforth more plainely yt doth &
may appeer. *fforma proclamaconis.*

Blackmoor Stannar'

Opus Stannar'	*Ad cur' predict tent apud*
vocat St Agnes	*Lostwithiall xiith dei Aprilis*
25 *Beame alias Holy*	*anno Regni d'ne n'r'e Elizabeth*
Roodwork.	*dei gratia Anglie ffranc'*
	et Hibernie Regine fidei
	defensoris etc xx veneru'
	Johes Dinham Nichus Stan=
30	*way et Petrus Nance et*
	dixerunt se bundasse opus
	stannar' p'dict sexto die Mar
	tii anno p'dict bunde incipi
	ent in orientali p'te curu'
35	*Pasle Poole in p'te australi*
	cum opere stannar' vocat
	Wellicaugh

In p'te Occidentali cu(m) bundis oper' stannar'
vocat Goodluck et in p'te boriali cu(m) comn'ne(?comune)
via d'n'e n're' Regine ducent a villa de Austell
versus Graumpond sicut bunde et limites in
seillic habent.

5

Off Corrupt tyn & of blo= wers of white tin.

All blowers of white tyn ought to appeer at
every law court at the stannary where they
10   blow their tyn & there by the Steward of the
court to have an othe ministred unto them that
they shalnot assent to the making of
any corrupt metalls so that every one of these ought
to have upon them there severall letters. which
15   must be set overthwart the peece of tyn contrary
to the blowing house marke & Awners of the tyn
mark hard tyn must have this letter H. Sinder
tyn the letter S. Pillion tyn this letter P. then is
there another kind of tynn worse then any of
20   this tynne called relistian tynne which
must have upon yt this letter R. theis 4 marks
of corrupt tyn every owner of a blowing
house ought to have in a redines at their blo=
wing howses.

25   Owners of blowing howses.

Every owner of a blowing howse ought to
present the names of their blowers with
Presentment yf they do omitt, & not present into the
Court book of the stannary upon the law day then
30   must the owner of the howse himself pay the
blowers amerciaments for his default of not
appeering at the Court, yf the owner of the
howse do present into the Court the names of
theire blowers & the blowers appeer not upon
35   the law day then goeth the amarcements out upon
the blowers.

Owners of blowing howses & makers of white Tynne.

As well all the owners of blowing houses as
the makers of white tyn ought to have their
markes as well of the blowing houses as of
the marks of the makers of white tyn to be

5   registred into the Court bookes of the stannary
which on thos dayes is negligently observed so that
great Complaints have risen of late dayes
by the Marchants for the sale of the tyn beyond
the seas being there fownd corrupt & having not
10   the accustomed letter appointed to be upon yt for
some kind of hard tyn having this letter H. upon
yt wilbe sold as soone as the mild & Marchantable
tyn abating only of the price xvjd or xxd
in the hundred.

15   How the Marchant taking lost
              in Sale of Corrupt tyn may
              be answered of his losts.

If any Marchant buying whit tyn & traveling
with his tyn beyond the seas or in any other place
20   chance to have trouble for corrupt tyn & selling
the same for soft pure & marchantable tyn not having
the markes of corrupt tyn & so by that meanes suff=
er great lost in the sale thereof he must cut out
the marke of the owner of the blowing house &
25   also the marke of the owner of the said tynne
being fownd corrupt which marks being brought
home, he first findeth out the blowing house
marke, then fyndeth he the marke of the said
tyn by his marke & so by theis meanes he get=
30   teth knoledge as well of the maker of
white tyn as the blower.

              That the blower is most blame=
              worthy of corrupt tynne
              without his letter.

35   At the last law court holden at Lostwithiall
in the xxviiith day of Aprill 1586. this
              question was

Preferred forth to be resolved of the custo=
mers of the stannary of Blackmoor sworne
for the Quenes majesty. concerning the said corrupt
tyn. A marchant selling his tyn beyond the
5   seas or on this side is troubled for corrupt
tyn, He cutteth out the markes, he bringeth
them home, he complayneth and setteth forthe
his greifes to the Court, the owner of the blo=
wing house being called by process cometh forth
10   into the court, so doth the owner of the tyn that
sold yt to the marchant, the blowers likewise
appeer in court, the markes of the tyn that is to
say both of blowing house and owner of the tyn
is there shewed and fownd corrupt which of all thes
15   being culpable ought to restore the marchant of
his lost & it was answered the blowers were most
worthy. ffor the owner of the howse cannot be
giltie of this offence for he suffereth straungers
sometime unknowen unto him to mak white
20   tyn in his blowing howse & never looketh to their
tyn whether it be corrupt mettall or not as
that hath sufficiently inough to do of his owne
busines & not intermeddle him selfe with the affairs
of other men being left of his care. The owners
25   of the tyn for his excuse allegeth that he bought
the black tyn & hath not the skill to know the
tyn being black whether it be corrupt
or not corrupt, as indeed the most conningst
tynner of all cannot discerne the false mettall
30   being black, therefore needs it must fall out that
the blowers ar in most default for they can by no
way excuse them selves for if it so fall out that
both the owner of the blowing howse & the maker
of the white tyn & twenty persons more were assent
35   together in the making of this corrupt tyn yet the
blowers of this tyn must needs be most faultie of all
others & therefore best worthy to restore the march=
chant of his lost.

What measures they have to
meet the tin in Blackmoor.

The tynners of Blackmoor most comonly
have two measures to meet their tin withall that
5   is to say a foot measure & a quart measure which they
comonly call a foot fate & a quart fate, the quart is
the fourth part of the foot. Both of theis ar used at every
delivery or washe made of black tyn, the foote mea=
sure (for I myself have mett him by a true quart
10   of Winchester measure) is five gallons & a pottle
of Winchester measure so then yt followeth that the quart
measure being the fowrth part of the foot must needs
be two quartes & a pint both of thes measures do
they use at every washe or delivery of black tyn for
15   this purpose, for they set abrod their tyn with the foot
fate as long as one foot or more feet will come by the
great measure to every tinners portion. And when
in meeting the tin falleth to be so litle in quantitie
as the latter end of meeting that they cannot be aun=
20   swered every one a foot of tyn for his part, then
they meat about the residue of the tyn with the litle
measure being the quart.

How the Tynners of the stannary of
Blackmoor meet their tyn.

25   Now in the stannary of Blackmoor only & none
other stannary they have this order. they will provide
one pickt out from the tynners at large if they
have none of their fellow workers can serve their
turn which can set tyn into the measure after the
30   lightest sort. this fellow shall have a place made
for him to syt upon directly hard against the heape
of tyn where the meater is set in his place he tak=
eth the foot or quart fate in his hands & settethe
him so ashoring wise that he shall hold halfe
35   his fill of water for the buyers of the black
tyn wilbe there & crave of Custome to have the
measure so be set, then the meater will take
out of the heap of tyn in his two hands
joyned together

Certaine tyn & so softly trinkell out the tynne
through his fingers litle & litle into the foot fate so
that he filleth the foot fate with as light measure as he
can untill the foot fate be so full as that the striker
5   which is a flat peece made of winscot or hart of oke
& bownden with iron made even for the purpose may
with striking over the measure touch the tyn along
over & over the measure which measure with the tyn in
hyt being set downe upon his bottome the tynne
10   will sinke downe a great way. this kind of mea=
ting is aswell liked of the buyer as
of the seller of black tyn, for I heard skilfull
tynners report that the foot measure being packt
hard will hold five quartes of tynne being met
15   of light measure as before is writen. this measure
of moor tyn being this mett after the lightest sort will
acquite himself well inough if it be of the best black
streame worke tyn, for they are of opinion that eight
foot of this measure will make two hundred & fiftie
20   powndes of white tyn & discharge the blowing besides
surely in myne opinion the tynners were better to
packe their tyn in the measure as fast as may be
packed. ffor then whereas the owner of black
tyn selling his tyn to the marchant making
25   white tyn for and after the rate of vd. ob the
marke every foot of black tyn as they comonly use
to do if it be of the best sort of black tyn receave
for every foot after the price of xxv li the thousand
of white tyn xvs.vijd.ob as falleth out after that
30   price. Now if their tyn be melt & made packt or
dagge measure they should then have by the said
price of xxv li the thousand for every foot of their black
tyn xixs.vjd.quarta.And this they putting all
men out of suspicion of deceipt of their light
35   measure should not only please the maker of
white tyn which buyeth the black tyn at their hands
but they should please God most chevest of all
which is the gever & preserver of all good things not with=
standing in deed the deceipt of this light measure
40   falleth not owt to him that maketh it white for the meating
of this principall good moor tyn that I spake of
before.

But the deceipt only of light meating fallethe
out in the light mine tyn in meating whereof
there is no doubt but the buyer whereof must
needs take great losts & that for the most part in the
5   making thereof white the lost thereof I my
selfe have felt or now to my great hinderance
this far have I writen for the meating of
tynne, not thinking the contrary but that the tynne
workers of Blackmoore wilbe much offendid
10   with me for my mocion as surely as they have none
occasion so as to be for when I have heard this
question moved unto them in the Court by the
steward they never liked the mocion much lesse those
minded to accept the same.

15   Diverse masters delivering out
their mony upon white Tynne
or black to the poor tynner
or spaliar not able to satisfye
who of the masters shall have the tynne.

20   If a poor man set mony upon his tyn with divers
masters before hand, which masters coming to the washe or conag
to receive of the poor man the tyn that they have
bought, every man clayming to have the poor mans tyn
which happely is not able to satisfye one of his masters
25   for the mony that he hath paid in this controversie
that master that the poor man assentith to deliver his
tyn unto shall have the tyn & the other masters
ar driven to seek their mony or tin for it by
way of asking.

30   Off Coliers & Cole Cariers.

Among the Tynners the coale burners & coale
cariers ar not to be forgotten for no man can
make his tyn white without the use of coale and
therefore ar they to be accomptid among the number
35   of tynners for the occupacion of the one cannot
wel stand without the other the colier craveth
by custome to have free pasturing of & for his
               horses.

In the carying of his coale peradventure xxx
or xl miles more or lesse to be pastured and
kept by them at their resting tyme in such
Comens & wast ground as they passe by toward
5   the blowing howses.

How much there Cole packs ought
to be.

Every Coale pack ought to hold in measure
three busshels xxtie gallons the busshell that is
10   to say one hogshed being a Burdeaux caske,
which may be well tryed by the coale pack him
self, for the pack must be in length two yerds
& one quarter of a yerd & in bredth three
quarters folding in & all so that one quarter is
15   alwais allowed for the knitting of their coale
packes being filled. whereupon yt hath bin seen
that the auncient tyn marchants would alwaies
have at there blowing howses a lawfull hogshed
the one end being striken out. then when the
20   coliers happened to come to the blowing house
with their coale, they would empty every pack
into the caske which measure was then fownd lawfull
if he filled the caske: if not the pack should be de=
faced as unlawfull measure & after not to be
25   allowed until he were amendid.

Off aresting tin that is in
striffe betwene partie & partie.

The baylife of the stannary or els the toller in the
baylifes absence hath full powre & authoritie to
30   arest any black tyn being in striffe betwene party
and partie & being upon the sheet ready to be delivered
& the same to comitt to honest & indiferent persons to
be safely kept in mean hands untill the contencion
betwene the said parties be pacified & the partie that
35   hath best right to the tyn being in strife fownd out
which tryall if it happen to belong, the bayliffe or the
toller (which arestid the tyn) upon request of either
of the parties being greived may bring the
matter

Returning it into the court bookes the better &
sooner there to be discussed betwene them & for the
spedier remedy to be had to the partie aggreved.

What remedy the owner of the
blowing house hath for tyn which is
blown at his howse and not paid for.

5

Now when the black tyn is made white then
it behoveth the same tyn to be caried straight to
the coynage & there with the Quenes hamer to be
coyned. So that if the maker of the white tyn be
a poor man & cannot pay for the charges of blo=
wing of his tyn: in this case the owner of the
blowing howse canot arest or so much stay the
white tyn at his blowing howse for the coale
blowers wages & the blowing thereof: But
for remedy of his mony he may lawfully
cause the steward of the coynage to keep &
retaine the bill of tyn after it is coyned untill
tyme that the owner of the blowing howse be paid for
the coale & blowing of this tyn otherwise he may
recover yt by accion of debt in the stannary
court against the maker of the white tyn if he be
sufficient.

10

15

20

The Custome of the Toller come
not to his hower to the delivery of
black tynne.

25

When the tynner hath purified his
tyn & brought yt to the sheet in a readines to
be delivered yt behoveth him to geve him law=
full warninge (the toller) of one or two dayes before he
intendeth to make his washe or more or les as the
dwelling of the toller & the tyme requireth so that
if the toller assent & grant to any hower of
delivery of the black tyn & come not to his houre
appointed (then as they say) they may lawfully
proceed in meating there
tynn.

30

35

And when the toller cometh out, then to set it upon
a greene turfe there to remaine the tollers co=
ming, for it may chance the owner of the blowing
house to sustaine great losse & hinderance for want
5   of black tyn to serve his hearth all which losse may
chance through slackness of the toller.

Off the fees of the gaole.

Among other things I may not forget the lamenta=
ble estate of the poor prisoners in remayning in the
10   gaole, or abroad at maine prison in the gaolers
custody. Now touching that matter at the law court
holden for Blackmore in the 28 day of Aprill
last past viz *anno domini* 1586. A question was pre=
ferred by bill to the Jurats being of the cheife
15   customers of tynners sworne for the Queene
at that court to be resolved by the verdict what
the fees of the gaole is that ought to be paid to the
keeper at the bringing in of a prisoner they pre=
sentid in their answere that the keeper ought to
20   have at the bringing in of a prisoner vjd. and
every day that he remayneth in the gaole and at the
keepers finding the prisoner must pay him iijd. every
day that the prisoner goethe at large & at the kepers
finding the prisoner must pay him vd. to be found
25   prisonerlike, but if the prisoner list to fare gen=
tilmanlike at the kepers table then must he pay there
after, but if he list to find him selfe at large in the
towne geving suretie to the keeper for his true impri=
sonment & considering the keeper somewhat for that
30   libertie yt were charitably done of him without
excesse of charges upon the the poor man, but if
the prisoner remaine in gaole & list by help of
his frinds to be at his owne finding in this

Case the keeper of the gaole ought to have nothing
for the gaole fees more than the vjd. which he paid
at his bringing into the gaole farther the prisoner
may be at the keepers finding in the gaole as longe
5   as he list & when soever his pleasure shalbe he
may return & be at his owne finding being in the
gaole.

Of the Spalier working for another
where he ought to be impleaded.

10   No man ought to comence or prosecute any accion
in the stannary court against the spalier or poore
workman which worketh anothers right in the tynn=
work being in strife but alwais he ought to
take his remedy by accion against the ow=
15   ner of the right.

No black tyn ought to remaine
unblowne after Michelmas day.

All maner of black tyn washid gathered and
made cleane ought to be blowen and made white before
20   the day and feast of St Michaell tharchangle
yerely.

No tynner for tyn matters ought
to assent to the tryall of the same
in a forraine Court.

25   If any tynner do voluntaryly appeer in any
forraine court for matters determinable in
the stannary court & standith there to his tryall
without pleding the accustomed plea of tyners
for the breach of the libertie in his defence, ought
30   to be presentid in the stannary court & to pay a
fine for his said offence as for formes sake I have
hereunto annexed the tynners answere in a
forren court to be impleaded in bar of that accon
laid against him.

35

The answere of a
tynner in a forren court.

And the aforesaid people came in their own persons
and defended the force and injury, etc, And they say that
there is a special law
within the whole stannary of the Duchy of Cornwall both by
diverse lord kings of England and forefathers of the lady Queen
5   now Duchess conceded to the said tinners, And by
that same Lady Queen to the same tinners
ratified and confirmed that no tinner of the lady Queen
shall reply to any justices or ministers
of the lady Queen or her heirs for any pleas
10   or quarrels arising within the aforesaid stannary
except in the presence of the warden of the stannary of the said
Queen of the aforesaid
tinners at that time except in pleas of land
of life and of limb nor withdrawing from their works
through the summons of any minister
15   of the said lady Queen or her heirs except through the summons
of the said warden of the said lady Queen
and to the care of the warden of the stannary in stannary court
and nowhere else just as is conceded to the tinners through that
same charter
that is more fully clear and apparent, And because of
20   this the aforesaid querent has spoken against the aforesaid
defendant in this court of and for the title and possession of that same
tin work called Losawork and for any
other trespass in the said tin work made
or perpetrated which are required to be determinable
25   or determined in the stannary court in the presence of
the stannary warden or his deputy or his lieutenant
there and in no other court of the said lady
Queen or of others where they seek of judges if
they wish to speak further than that court, etc

30   One Tynner ought not to implead
                 another out of the stannary court
                 for matters there determinable.

If one Tynner do implead another in any
forren court & both of them do assent to
35   have the matter tryed in a forren court
the matter being in the stannary court de=
terminable, both of them ought to be pre=
sentid for breach of there libertie for the
party being aggreved as well the deff=
40   endant

Lines 1-29 translated from Latin.

As the plaintiff may have his remedy in the stan=
nary court by way of accon or otherwise.

No *replevin* ought to be sued out
of the stannary Court for tyn causes.

5   Not only tynners but also forreners ought by
the Custome for tyn matters to sue out ther
replevins at the hands of the Lord Warden of the
stannary or his deputy in the stannary where
as the matter is Determinable the doers
10 of the Contrary ought to be presentid into
the said stannary for breach of the Custome.

Tynners impanelled in Juries.

No Tynner ought to be impanelled in any
Jury other for the Queens majesty or els betwene
15 party and party except only in the severalle
Division of the stannary Court wher he dwel=
leth.

One having right in a tinworke
going about to deceive the rest
20 of his fellowes.

There hath bin a Custome amongst tinners that
whereas divers owners ar seised of & in one
Tynworke together, one of the owners goeth
about to deceive all his partners by pollicie
25 bringing theire work vacant to that intent to bring
the work into his owne hands or els into
the hands of lesse number of owners this
fellow entring in with the new pitchers of
this work by the Custome bringeth in all the
30 residue of the old owners. for if it can be
proved that one old owner have right with the
new pitchers the right of that one bringeth
in all the other. But now they have devised
a pollecie to bar this, for when the old owner
35 receiveth his right with the new pitchers

He shall not have the right him self but it
shalbe geven to his sonne his daughter or som
other frind of his so that nothing shalbe assigned
to him of all his right. this without doubt is
5   a very great deceipt & of all other things worthy to
be redressed. Offten tymes they will not stick
to geve a good part of the right to a gentleman, or a
lawier to support them in their crafty dea=
lings which is very well preventid & lookt to a=
10   mongst the tynners of Devon for there, if
any one of them go about to defraude his
coopartners & suffereth the work to be lost not
geving his fellowes warning thereof before
that then the tynner going about his deceite
15   shall straight way lose his right to the said
worke to the use of his partners and the
new pitcher shall forfait xx li. the one half
to the prince & the other half to them that
shalbe so defrauded yf it be fownd by ver=
20   dict of xij men a *fyeri facias* to be a=
warded as well. for the prince as for the party.

Of a Nichill in the Court
and a *distringas.*

Concerning Nichels in the Court this hath bin the old
25   auncient order that when the accion is entred into
the Court, the baylife being asked whether the
defendant be suficient to answere the plaint of his der(?)
yf he be able the bayliffe then taking, vjd. for
his fees, he must warne the defendant to answere
30   the complent in his accon at the court insuing so
the defendant at that court making default a
Distringas is grantid against him to distraine
his goods to bring him into the Court then next
after the Distringas so graunted out to answere
35   the plaintiff in his accion the plaintiff alwayes paying
to the court for his princes vjd. to the bayliff

And to the bayliffe for serving the same vjd.
If the defendant Do then againe make default in
answering the plaint there ensueth out of the court
an *alias distringas* & so consequently a *plu=*
5   *res distringas* alwayes dubling such a grea=
vous amercement distress thereupon gran=
tid untill the defendant come to his answere
as the steward thinketh good to set upon the defendant
for his over great contumacie. Now if the
10   baylife thinke the defendant not sufficent
to answere the plentiff in his action, then
doth he Nichill the defendant whereupon
there ensueth out a write which they call a warrant to
arest the defendant by the body compelling him to
15   geve sureties to answere the plaint of his demand.
Now for as much as the bayliffes having there
process delivered to them to arest the defendant for
the most part do not observe truly the tenour of theire
process, therefore have I thought it good somewhat
20   to touch the same. ffor the wordes of their process
are that they should bring the defendant before the
steward there to take suretie to answere the plea
which although it be mentioned in the write yet they
omit to do taking sureties them selves, this in
25   very deed hath bin both used and allowed
for lawfull tyme out of mind aswell of the
steward as of the plaintiff & defendant. And upon
the othe of the Bayliffe being sworne at the
Court then next, that he arestid the defendant by the
30   body whereupon such a man and such became
the defendants sureties that he should personally
appeer naming him sureties & to answere the
said plaint in his said accon. Now if the Defendant come
not in personally at any one court of three cour=
35   tes then next ensuing & answere the plaintiff accordingly.

The defendant is then by Custome condemned to pay
unto the plaintiff his due debt together with damages
costs & charges which shalbe tasked by two in=
different tynners in the court presently to be
5   returned, for the lyvying where of the steward
maketh out his *fieri facias* aswell against the
defendant as his sureties for the satisfaction of the
debt to the plaintiff together with his expenses &
damages besides. And because I have thought
10   yt most necessary in this place to be annexed
I have hereafter placed first the forme of a
distringas grauntid out of the court for him
that is fownd sufficient then of a warrant
against him that is adnihiled lastly the form
15   of a wryte of *fieri facias.*

The forme of a Distringas.

Walter Raleigh knight, guard,
warden and chief steward of our lady
Queen for her Duchy of Cornwall to the bailiffs of the tinners
20   of Blackmoor and also P.D., etc, of them whatsoever.
Greetings to you and I order that any of you shall distrain
or one of you shall distrain of J.C.
on all of his own land goods and chattels
to the value of 8d. to the use of the said our lady
25   Queen if the aforesaid John Coryn does not personally
appear at the next stannary court aforesaid
held next after the date of these presents to answer
one G.A. in a plea of debt just as is recorded in the stannary court
aforesaid more plainly clear and apparent
30   And thay shall have or one of them shall have with them then
and there, viz, at the next court aforesaid this mandate
given with this transaction and this no-one may omit
nor any of them omit under the penalty
as obliged and given under the seal of office of the Duchy
35   aforesaid day and year, etc.

Lines 17 to end of page translated from Latin.

The forme of a Warrant.

Walter Raleigh knight, guard, warden
and chief steward of our lady Queen in her Duchy
of Cornwall, to the bailiffs of the stannaries of Blackmoor,
Foymoor, Penwith, Kerrier and Trywarnhale
5   and also F.R. and any others whatsoever, Greetings, if J.S.
has made you or one of you surety for his claim
to prosecute against N.L. in a plea of trespass in which case
he has nothing, for which on behalf of our lady Queen to you and
any of you, I order that you make the aforesaid defendant come
10   into the presence of my deputy assigned for that purpose, to
provide sufficient surety to reply to the next
stannary court within B. aforesaid held next after the date of these
presents, to reply to the aforesaid quarrel in his plea aforesaid,
And if he should refuse to do this then take him
15   or one of you take him and detain him at the gaol of our said
lady Queen made at Lostwithiel in the Duchy
there and for any who should wish to do this favour
I also send to you as warden of the gaol aforesaid
to keep the said body received into your gaol
20   and guard it there safe and sound for which
delivery you have sufficient warrent in these
orders, And this no man of you may ignore under the penalty
incumbent, Given under the seal of the office of the Duchy
aforesaid of God and in the year, etc.

25   The forme of the writ of *fieri facias*

Walter Raleigh knight, etc, On behalf of our lady
Queen, to you and whichever of you I order and firmly
enjoin that you cause to have made or one
of you causes to have made from his own goods and chattels of J.
30   N. as a fine of 30s. and 10s. namely, for myself, and
expenses so that you have money ready in the
next stannary court aforesaid, held next after the
date of these presents to the satisfaction of R.H. for the
recovery by the same against the aforesaid J.N. in that same
35   court held in a certain plea of trespass upon a case of if you
possess otherwise that you take the aforesaid defendant through
his body and lead him that has been taken
to the gaol of the lady Queen at Lostwithiel
made for the Duchy there to keep him for

Line 2-24 & lines 26 to end of page translated from Latin.

the satisfaction of the recovery aforesaid, And if the money
for the goods of the said defendant that you cause to have taken
are not enough, and his body you do not find, then the money that
you cause to have taken for goods and chattels of John Doe and
5   Richard Roe, who agreed to act as bail and body for the defendant,
for the said pledge, be taken and led to the gaol of our said Queen
in aforesaid Duchy, made for the aforesaid recovery of the
satisfaction just as has been written above and send also to the
warden of the gaol aforesaid that when the body of the aforesaid
10 defendant or his pledge have been taken and led to you, that you
receive him into the said gaol and keep him safe and that for that
delivery you have sufficient warrant in these orders, And this
no man may ignore under the standing penalty, Given
under seal of the Duchy office aforesaid, etc.

15   The Right of Tynworkes descendeth
                to the Executors.

If any man dye being possessed of lands and
tinworkes as by the lawes of the Realm the fre=
hold of the land alway descendeth to his heires
20 even so the freehold of the Tynworkes descendeth
by the Custome to the Executors of the defunct.

                Of collections of mony to be made
                for the confirmacon of the Charter
                of tynners or els other duties con=
25   cerning them.

When a collection of a sum of mony is to be
gathered for the confirmacon of the Charter of
tynners or for redress of causes touching stannary
matters as fell out by Brokehouse whereof mention is made before
                pagination or such other
30 like matter concerning tynne. thus hath bin the
only way as far as ever I have knowen the Lord
warden his vice warden deputie or substitute
being moved into this collection by request of the
tynners causeth precepts to be sent to the Consta=
35 bles of every severall parishes whereas tynners ar comon at
commanding them to be at the next stannary
court of ther division & then & there to bring in
a true certificate by writing of every worker
spaliar laborer or mellor
40   with

Lines 1-14 translated from Latin.

With tyn of their parishe. this certificate being
diligently done, then by conference together of the
officers of the fowre severall Courts amongst
them selves & they find out the sume how much it
5   ought to be that shalbe needfull to be collectid
and so knowing the numbre of the tinners con=
sidering likewise how this sume will be raysed upp
whether it be ijd. every tynner more or lesse.
then ar the Constables of every parishe comandid
10   to gather it up & bring it to the handes of some
one appointid to receive it at such day time &
place as the expedicon of the case requirethe
to use the mony collectid for the Constables
men that know best the tynners that know the waies
15   & meanes how to levy this sum in their severall
parishes. And surely I never perceived otherwise
but they have alwaies obediently used this
service. I have known another way for this coll=
ection to be made for tyn causes which hath bin
20   used upon the white tyn at the Quoynage
and that surely is the most surest way, but in ray=
sing of this collection the master receiver of Corn=
wall must be made privye with all to whose hands
all the bills of tyn do come which in receaving
25   the Queens custome at the setting out of the tyn may
likewise receave this ratement with all that is to
say upon every thousand of white tyn to receave
at the hands of every owner of every bill to sum which by the ra=
ters of that collection shalbe by appointment
30   thought good & then the whit tyn marchants to
accompt with the sellers of black tyn which collection
of right great sumes I have known to be lyvied
& taken up after this order & as truly justly
satisfyed ever. thus much have I writen for a
35   collection of a sum of mony to be made for tyn
causes. But if this collection of mony must
be made for service of our prince to have

myners spaliars or pyners not only to work for
her grace but for the defence & safegard of us all
I daresay that there is no indifferent gentleman yeoman
or true subject that will otherwise judge, but that
5   theis our generall servants the pioners I mean
which doth Jeopard their lyves & bestow their ser=
vice for our helth safegard & comoditie of us all
and in that respect ought to be set forth with the charge
generally as well of parishes that have no tynners
10   as of parishes that have tynners.

        The Coopartners of tynners ought
        to be diligently warned to come to
        the washe.

All captayne owners of tinworkes when they
15   go about to make theire washe ought to geve
lawfull warning to their coopartners which have
borne the charges with them in working of their
tyn, for doing whereof the captaine of the work
is to be charged if the said coopartner so to be warned
20   have in the said work his hired man or spaliar
then the warning to the spaliar or hired man
of the said coopartner so geven is sufficient to
the discharge of the said captaines of the tyn
worke, yf the captaines of the tynwork omit to
25   do their duties in this respect they ought to be
presentid in the court.

        A tynner be seised of right in a tyn
        worke one yeer & a day peaceably can
        not be avoyded but by law only.

30   If any person or persons be peaceably seased and
possessed of a tynwork or any part of a tynwork
by the space of one yeer & a day no man ought
by the custome to enter upon the said right be his
title never so good untill the said title be fully
35   tryed & determined betwene the said parties
by order of the Lord Warden or his deputie
of the stannaries which shall grant out his in=
junction upon a paine by him to the party
offending geven to avoid from perturbing

-51-

The possessioners right as for orders sake I have
annexed hereunto one forme of a declaration
to be impleaded in court for the like offence.

A declaration for trespasse against
5   one entring upon ther peaceable
possession of another.

John B. is distrained to reply to T.R. in
a plea of trespass, And thence the plaintiff in his own person
has appeared and says that it is the custom within
10   the stannary of B. used and proved beyond the
the memory of man to which it is not contrary, that no-one
makes an entry on any tin works in the possession
of a tinner of our lady Queen where the aforesaid tinners
have possession peacefully and legitimately of the site
15   of their said works through a space
of a year and a day, And if anyone
has an entry upon the possession of any tinners of
our said lady Queen against custom
aforesaid by the steward of the said lady Queen
20   may be removed until his right and title between
the parties following the custom and law of the aforesaid stannary
have been discussed, should however, the aforesaid J.B. have a title
of a day
and a year by force and arms, viz, with shovels, forks and
pickaxes in one tinwork belonging to this
25   plaintiff being empty of a dole of tin at G. within
the jurisdiction, etc, upon possession of the said plaintiff
against the custom of the stannary aforesaid
Blackmoor, and the said plaintiff for the peaceful possession
promised to them, and there seize it back and
30   expel(them), and the man thus de-seised expel by the aforesaid
statement until, etc, with such kinds of force, power and
manufacture held out and still holds out
and other irregularities brings himself into contempt
of the said lady Queen to the serious detriment of the plaintiff
35   and against the peace of the said lady Queen from which the said
defendant
has been condemned and has a fine to the value of 40
and thence to produce a suit,etc.

Line 7 to end of page translated from Latin.

ffreehold pled in court to bar
the plentyve of his action.

If any accon of trespas be brought by any tiner
for trespas done in his grownd. And the defendant come=
5   ing into court pleadeth in bar of the action
that the place whereas the trespas is supposed to
be done in his freehold or els the freehold of
another person and prayeth to be dismissed for
as much as it is concerning land the steward
10   in this case shall geve him day at the next court
to bring his writing, of the writing of him
whose he supposeth the frehold to be or credi=
ble witnes that he or the persons in whom he sup=
poseth the freehold to be were seased of the fre=
15   hold at tyme of the trespas against him sup=
posed whereby the freehold may appeer to him
or them that then upon this proves made the
defendant shalbe dismissed at the discretion of the
steward yf not to make answere at his perill.

20   How Tinworkes should be disposed.

There are three maner of wayes to geve tyn
workes, that is to say by Testament by letter of a=
turny & hand delivery but this note cheifly
that if he geve divers workes lyvery must pas
25   in every work.

             Appellacons by severall degrees
             out of the stannary Court.

If any Tynner be Wronged he must seek for
redresse of his wrongs if the case require
30   so by severall appellacons as first he ought
to complaine to the steward of the stannary court
where the matter lyeth next to the under war=
den of the stannaryes & for want of justice
at his hands to the Lord Warden of the stannaries
35   fynally if he then canot have redresse he must
complaine to the princes privy Counsell and
             not

And not examinable in any other court as
by a certaine decree grantid out of the Starr
Chamber by the most Honorable Counsell of the xxixth
of Novembre *Ao.Regni Dom'ne nostre* Elizabeth
5   *nunc Regine etc vii* concerning a matter
in variance betwene Martin Trewennard
plantiff & John Reskarrack and other defendants
more playnly it doth and may appeer the
Coppye of which decree hereafter follo=
10   weth word for word.

            Off the writes of error that
            Martin Trewinnard esquire
            had from the Quenes benche
            and the Copie of the decree
15   of the Star Chambre:
            xvth die Junii Ao.Regni Elizabeth Regine
            iiii. inter Mart.Trewinnard
            a cur' stannar' in Com' Cornub' dcf.

Whereas Martin Trewinnard Esquire hath
20   proceeded forth of this court two severall writs
of Error returnable in the Queen's bence and
there upon hath orderly proceedid unto the alias
& pluries upon the same writes of error the
one betwene the said Martin Trewinnard
25   and one George Trewinnard & the other betwene
one John Kellygrew the said Martin & one
Richard Scaddion & others defendants which se=
verall writes of error were directed unto the
Lord of Loughborough Steward & Warden of the
30   stannaryes of Cornwall & Devon & to his ste=
ward & under steward & bayliffes of the
stannary court of Penwith & Kerrier in the
said Court of Cornwall which severall writs
the said Lord of Loughborough warden of the
35   sayd Stannaryes nor his said officers of
the Stannary court nor any of them
               hath hitherto

Duke of Cornwall's Coat of Arms carved on the front of the Convocation Hall, Duchy Palace, Lostwithiel.

Photograph *Royal Institution of Cornwall*

Certifyed according to the contents of the
same writes to them directid for that behalfe where
upon the same Martin Trewinard moving this
court thereof hath already desired to have attache=
5   ments upon the same severall contempts against
the said warden & his officers of the said court
according to the order of the law in that behalfe. And
whereas also the said plaintiffs in the said writes of error
are presintid in the same tyncourt at the procure=
10   ment of the same warden & his officers for
prosequuting of the said writes of error to thintent
greavously to aver & to set & taske fines & amerci=
aments upon the plaintiff in the said writes of error
It is now ordered therefore by this court that the said Lord
15   of Loughborough warden of the said stannaries &
his deputes for the time being shall shew forth in this
court the first day of the terme of St Michaell next
coming the liberties & charters of the said stannarye
court & also to shew sufficient & lawfull cause and
20   matter why they have not or ought not to have
certified the said severall writes of error accor=
ding to the tenor of the same or els attachements upon
the contempts of the said severall writes of error
is & ar to be awarded. And also yt is further orday=
25   ned that the said plaintiff in the said writes of error
nor any of them be not in the same mean tyme
disquietid molestid stayd or arestid by any of
the said judgements or executions given or
to be geven against them or any of them in the
30   said stannary court but that the same court &
the severall plaintiffs in the said severall actions there
shall & do also sursease & stay the same severall
judgements & execute there in upon the like
payne of contempt out of this court to be awar=
35   ded. And also further it is ordered that the said Lord
of Loughborough warden of the said stannary
nor any his stewards deputs & officers of
the same court shalnot from henceforth further
proceed to or in any presentments therupon to averse
40   the same Martin Trewaynnard & other the plaintiff
in the same writes of error for pursuing the
same

-55-

Writes untill for this order by this court in
that behalfe upon the like damage of attachements
to be also awarded.

William Naylor.

5   In Star Chamber in the presence of the Council there, Wednesday
    29th November in the seventh year of the reign of our lady
    Elizabeth, Queen, Defender of the Faith.

    Where a matter of variance hath bin heretofor
    moved & depending on this honorable court be=
10 twene Martin Trewynnard plaintiff & John Reskar=
    rock William Gilbart John Kellegrew the yonger
    James Drew & others defendid by two severall
    billes exhibited into this court, where of the last bill
    contayneth no other matters of effect being not
15 mentioned in the first bill other then the lak=
    ing of certaine cattle of the said complainant and
    others & where also yt appeereth this present
    day that the laking of the said cattle was by
    certaine of the defendants lawfully aucthorised
20 for that purpose by the steward of the stannary
    Court of Penwith & Kerrier in the Cownty of
    Cornwall for executions upon condemnacons
    by judgements had in the said court against the
    said plaintiff touching which Condemnacons the said
25 Complainant hath complayned as well in Court of
    Chancery by bill in the kings benche by write
    of Error as also in this court as appeereth
    in the prescript of the said two bills adheere
    depending meaning by some of theis waies
30 to call in question the validitie of the said judg=
    ment and was out of the said severall courts
    by order discharged and dismissed referring
    the proceedings upon the said judgement to the order
    of the said stannary court according to divers
35 ordinances by divers auncient charters customs
    & liberties belonging to the stannary ratified
    by act of parlyament & where it doth also appeer
    that the taking of the said cattle where upon
                    the said bill in this
40   Court

Lines 5-7 translated from Latin.

Is exhibited was only for the execution of the
said recovery. And where also it doth further appeer
that by the lawes & ordinances of the said stannary if
any such cause of complaint be ministred the same
5   is to be redressed by appellacons, in severall degrees
viz first to the steward of the stannary court where
the mater lyeth. then to the under steward of the stan=
naryes & from him to the Lord Warden of the said stan=
naryes. And for default of justice at his handes
10   to the princes privy Counsell & not examinable
either here in this court or in any other court. It is
therefore this present day ordered that the said se=
verall bills of complaint and the said defendant named
in the same with all the causes therein mentioned
15   be forthwith dismissed out of this court to be deter=
mined according to the lawes & ordinances in the
said stannary & not elswhere.

        Concordat cu' decret
        Curie Thome Marshe
20   Off the wages of tynners & spaliers
        & of their estate and habilitie.

The most part of the workers of black tyn and
spaliars are very poor men as men doubt
that occupacon can never make them riche & chefly
25   such tin workers as have no bargaines but only trust
to their wages although they have never so riche
a tynworke. for they have no profit of their tyn if they
be hyred men saving only their wages for their
masters have their tyn. Now if they should chance
30   to be farmers them selfes and their workings fall
bad, then run they most cheifly in their masters debt
& likely to increase more & more rather then
to acquite any part thereof. for of thes two choises
to be a hired man or a farmer the one is a cer=
35   tentie & the other an uncertentie the farmour
knoweth not how his worke will do untill tyme
that he hath proved yt and must needs live in
hope all the yeer which for the most part deceiveth
him, as the saying is, *qui spe vivit agitam serum*
40   *agit vitam.*

Then on the other part concering the wages of the
tynner working his dole. the comon wages is
but iij li. or five markes a doles working for the
yeer to the uttermost & yet must the worker find
5   himself meat & drink which is litle above ijd. a day
this poor man happely hath a wife & iiij or v small
children to care for which all depend upon his
getting, whereas all his wages is not able to buy
himselfe bread, then to passe over the poor mans
10   howse rent clothing for his poor wife & children
besides diverse other charges dayly growing upon
them. O God how can this poor man prosper
yet this much must I confesse of the welthiest
company of tinners which happely worke together
15   in one tynworke with the poor man. they are
very charitable & mercifull toward their poor
fellow workers, for at dinner tyme when they
syt downe together beside their tynwork in a
litie lodge made up with turfes covered with straw
20   & made about with hansome benches to sit upon
then every tynner bringeth forth out of their
scrips or tynbags his victuals his bread his
bottle of drink as the riche tynners will lack
none being lest of them in numbre. then
25   is their charitie so great that if one two or 3
or els more poor men syt among them ha=
ving neither bread drink or other repast
there is not one among all the rest
but will distribute at the largest sort with their
30   poor worke fellowes that have nothing: so that in
the end this poor man having nothing to re=
leive him at the worke shall in fine be better
furnished of bread butter cheese beef pork
& bacon, then all the richest sort, yea the poor=
35   est of them all in this respect (if he have
yt) wilbe most desirest to geve, as the poor
widow that

Cast the two brasse pence to the value of a farthing
into the treasury most highly being comended of
our saviour Christ himselfe. this the poor man being
furnessed for his owne releife for the tyme may
5   carry the overplus toward the releife of his poor
family home with him.

Off the spale of tinners and their
usage there upon with intring into their work.

At the end of the yeer which tynners accompt to be
10   at Michelmas after the coynage, then they devise their
work consulting together how many doles they
shalbe which needs must be done in auncient tyn=
workes for the most part before the xviijth day of
October being St Lukes day, for upon the Monday
15   after that day they enter all together into their said
tynworkes. then after they have appointed one
of their company to be their captaine, this must
needs be such one of their company as worketh
a full dole theire, then make they a goad or rod
20   pared fowersquare being in length or shortness
according to the number of the workers. In this
goad every of theis fellow work tinners shall
have his severall places squatched out to
to him that they call their parckes so from that time
25   all the yeer after every fellow worker lacking
from his worke shalbe set upon his park iiijd.
for every day in spale that he lacketh, or els if he be
in another mans work or if it chance the wor=
kers that day to be troubled with much water as
30   often tymes they shalbe then the spale is vjd.
or more for in that service they shall often tymes
want help & will set the more spale upon the
lacker. Now if the fellow worker being lacke
chaunce to fall sick in his bedd, or so that he canot
35   go abroade, then shall his spale be but ijd.

Every day continuing the tyme of his sicknes
but if he be sick and able to come to his worke &
syt upon the borough all the day long although he
do nothing at all he shalbe nothing in spale
5   the like charitie they use amonge them that if one
of their worke fellowes although the sempelst
of them all fall sick at his worke, this fellow
shalbe cherised among them and the best bot=
tell of drink amongst them all shalbe sought
10   out for them yea aquavite or any good preser=
vative that may be gotton for mony which they com
by, shall speedely be sent for to comfort this sicke
man, And in conclusion they appoint diligent=
ly men to bring him home to his house if he be
15   not able to go himself with no lesse care then if he were
their father their brother or their naturall
child. Surely I suppose that theis charitable orders
among them geveth the poor men occasion to covet
to be workefellowes among them. thus they proceding
20   forthe in their working from time to tyme if any mony
lacke to the use of their working as to amend
their pikes to make their tackle to defend the
title of their tyn work by law or any other necessa=
ry use. then upon this occasion or the like they take
25   mony of some one that hath his right of his tinne
worke working over the whole company after the
wages of iij li. or five markes the dole by the yeer
of which there are sundry in that company. then
at the first beginning of June or neer there
30   about they prepare their washe to have theire
black tyn made white against midsomer conage
which black tyn being purified clensed dressed &
brought to the heap ready to be delivered, there
buddle & tyn stones which they call brewes & the rux
35   being sold to marchants called loppers or buddle
buyers which use to come to all tynworkes & washes
only for that purpose stamping & powing the said
brawes & Rux & therof they make black tyn
and by purifiinge

And dressing maketh it white wherby they have som
time greater gaines then the tynner himself
then the Captaine of the tynners setteth downe
& all his fellowes besides him he calleth for the
5   buddle mony, then for the hired mony over the
Company, next for the spale mony which all being
brought in & cast into a sive or searge then the
captaine demandeth who can aske anything for char=
ges bestowed about the said worke, one cometh
10   forth and demandeth for a sheet that he brought the tin
upon, another for a serrge another for a seive then
for the hire of the measures to meat their tyn with
all then for watching the tyn by night & for dress=
ing & purifying the same so falleth out in the end that
15   every demander is fully recompenced for his paines
and travell and all things lent to the use of the
worke considered which payment to the uttermost
of their whole demaund and the rest devided a=
amongst the owners every man his part.

20   Off the merry devises comonly used
             among tynners and of the termes
             of naming of thinges in
             theire tynworkes.

Iff I taking upon me to write
25   the Customes of Tinners as much as I can call
to remembrance, should omit & passe over with
silence any part of their old usages comonly practi=
sed amongst them I should then seeme to be negligent
in performing my promis. therefore as I have written
30   of the Customes together wth their charitie
used toward ther poor work fellowes so were it
necessary for me to write somewhat of their mirth
which they use without offence to any man. And that for
two principall causes, one is for that it shall recriat
35   the reader to have some merry toy ministred among
so many blont customes & usages for that the preacher
in his pulpit ministring to his auditors no de=
lectable history should happely bring his auditors
into a dead sleep, Another cause is for that yt
40   may so chance that some reading this my rude
simple & tynnerlike treatis and meaning to work

With tynners & to spend his life amongst them
may be reading thereof learn that which other=
wise they cannot attaine unto without some proces of
tyme. when it chancethe that an ignorant spalier
5   comethe to save any of theire fellowes for the tyme
then fall they to reason the matter within them
selfes very solemly & sadly as though it were about a matter
of gravitie one laying the fault upon another be=
cause they want their corde to meat their worke is
10   all, or els their barrow or such a like thing, then
one amongst the rest confesseth that such a day
(naming the day) they had their corde & lent him to such a worke
naming some tynwork hard by them, then this igno=
rant spalier which came that day to the worke to save
15   one of their worke fellowes shalbe sent to that work
to seek their corde or theire barrow. Now when he
cometh to that worke they perceiving the matter straight
way after much debating one with another why and
wherefore they should be so negligent to spare the
20   corde to another worke which they to their most need
have borowed yet in fyne sendeth him to the next
work thereby but this shalbe handled
among them with so great a grone & that
from one worke to another that the poor man going
25   from worke to worke although it were through the
whole stannary shall never understand the matter
but at last cometh home to the worke againe as
wise as he went forthe, yet among a number
of unskillfull spaliers they find some craftie
30   fellowes that match aright their merry devises
one of theis craftie fellowes pleading simpli=
citie being mocioned with them to fetch home their
cord & making a countenaunce to go forther in deed
getteth him out of their sight into a shadowed
35   place under some tree and there lyeth & sleepith
all the day long coming home to them when
               tyme is come to leave

There working and reherseth to them what travell
he hath taken all the day long wandring from one
tynwork to another as though he were cleaneweri=
ed out whereas all that while he hath done nothing
5 but loyter and sleep. Another merry devise they have
as this. when a gentilman or a husband man ha=
ving right working among them, happely sendethe
one servant of his house to save his hired tynwor=
ker for the day being occupied about other business
10 after tyme that it falleth late toword the even tyde, then
consult they together for deviding up ther tyn stones
which they call brawes so that every man must have
his porcion devided out, then gather they together
as many heapes of stones as they be workers in the
15 tynworke, appointing this gentelmans ser=
vant to chuse out his masters part of the
brawes because his master is a gentleman
& they would in no wise assent or seeme to
defraude him of his right the poor man mean=
20 ing good diligent service toward his master
& chusing the greatest heap of all the other,
which are nothing else but great black stones
without any good tyn good for no purpose &
to please his master the better one knave or an=
25 other geveth him of their part deafe stones
saying that they be very good tyn brawes which
the poor man taketh very thankfully & home
straight to his master goeth he heavely laden with
stones with his scrip bosome & breeches alstuft
30 up with black stones he when he cometh home
to his master bosteth to him of his good successe of
his tyn brawes & forthwith presenting them
the gentleman knowing the mery use of the
tynners prayseth very much his servants dili=
35 gence & comendeth him for a profitable ser=
vant. Now if it chance by occasion of talk
that one of the work fellowes bad another

Come kysh his arse then make they all a
great showte that it behoveth this fellow to have
his arse cleane washed that will have him to be
kissed, so to the the river this fellow is borne with
5   strength of the fellow workers for it is vaine
labour to strougle against them if he were
never so tall a fellow. adowne then ar his bre=
ches set & his arse saving your reverence well
plonged in the deepest place of all ther is
10   & insteed of a towell to wipe his tayle, one co=
meth with a scowpfull of gravell & litle rough
garde with this gard the poor mans tayle
shalbe so rubbed that the bloud shall follow & all
this they say must needes be done to make his
15   tayle cleane against that he shalbe kissed. the like
order they kepe If they hear say that any of ther
fellowes hath bin beaten with his wife then the
tynner that dwelleth next to him that is beaten shall
with strengh of his fellowes be borne to the water
20   & there plonged in the river. Another merry
devise they have which is knowen & used among
tynners throughout all the whole stannary
which is this when occasion of talke is ministred
that they must make mencion of owles foxes
25   hares catts cats or rats then it behoveth you
to beware cheifely for then must you speake in
tynners language & in none other language
then tynners have decreed, the owle must be
called a broadface, the fox a long tayle, the
30   hare a long yeer the cat a Rooker & the rat a
peeper. the tynners generally will of set pur=
pose sometyme minister such matter in their
talke that they will bring you to name some one
of thes yea some tyme the cuningst of them all
35   forgetting their termes or thinking of no such
matter may be deceaved so that if they name any
one of all theis as by the name of a fox not
calling him a longtayle

A cat or a rat not calling them a rooker and
a peeper or any such like. this fellow mysusing
his termes is a very haynous offender but in
no danger of death, nor yet pillory matter
5   but the offence is finable & ratid by the decree
of all the tynners of Blackmoor which is to pay
for a gallon of ale so this drinke shall spedely be=
set at the ale house and as merely drank
amongst them.

10   Off conveying of waters
             to the working of a foreyn(er).

The tynners have alwais accustomed to fet cary
and convey water to and from any tyn work
to the use of their working in over & through
15   any lords severals as of late dayes hath bin
fully tryed by the Errle of Bedfords tyme
when he was Lord Warden of the stannaries
the Records where of (as I believe) I shall get
before I fynishe this my booke.

20   Off the fees of any bayliffe
             of the stannary serving their proces.

Any bayliffe of the stannaries ought not to
take of any prisoner being arestid more
more then vjd. whether it be the cheif baylife
25   or the speciall bayliffs & that whether he be tyn=
ner which is arestid or foryner for the fees
thereof is all like.

             How the sellers of black tyn
             within this stannary of Blackmoor
30   do reckon with the makers of white
             tyn & what rule they have in ther
             price making.

In tymes past the comon price of white tyn
was xxiiij or xxv markes the thousand & very
35   often within that, as one yeer it was xiiij markes
the M li & fell above xxiii markes the next yeere
after because in thos auncient dayes the tynne was much
more plenteous then it is now in our tyme.

The tynners of Blackmoor used to make up
their accompt upon the black tyne with the buyers
thereof by the marke which custome they continue
forthe unto this day how soever the price fall up
5   or downe there recken falleth out in this
order look how many markes one thousand
of tyn is sold for according to the comon price
so many tymes vd. iiijd. ob. or iiijd more or lesse
according to the goodnes of your black tyn shall
10   you have for your foote of blacktyn as is loe, if
it be of the best Blackmoor tyn yt will bear vd.
every mark of the free tyn & none lightly above
that yf they set their mony before upon there
tyn then come they to a lesse price as they can
15   make their bargaine to be breif I have anexed
here unto a table of the rating of the price of
a foote of tyn by one marke of every thousand
from twenty pownds upward whereby you
shall the better understand the order of their
20   comen reckninges.

By this present table you may quickly fynd
out the prise of a foot of tyn after the mark
as tynners of Blackmoor stanary do comonly
recken, that is from xx li. the thousand to xxvij li. ac=
25   cording to the goodnes of the tyn that is from iijd.
the mark increasing the ob. upward till yt com
to vd.ob. the mark which is the highest price of
any black tyn sold within the stannary of Blac=
moor as after this sort, yf the tyn be sold
30   after iiijd.ob the marke the price of the thousand
being xxiiij li. guyd your sight from xxiiij li. the
price of the li and you shall find the foot
after iiijd.ob the mark to be xiijs.vjd.(13s.6d.)

The thowsand of tyn Being

The price of the foot after	Li xx	Li xxj	Li xxij	Li xxiij	Li xxiiij	Li xxv	Li xxvj	Li xxvij
iijᵈ the marke	vijˢ vjᵈ	vijˢ xᵈ ob	viijˢ iiijᵈ	viijˢ vijᵈ ob	jxˢ	jxˢ iiijᵈ ob	jxˢ jxᵈ	xˢ jᵈ ob
iiijᵈ ob the marke	viijˢ 9ᵈ	jxˢ ijᵈ ob qu	jxˢ vijᵈ ob	xˢ ob qu	xˢ vjᵈ	xˢ xjᵈqu	xjˢ iiijᵈ ob	xjˢ ixᵈ ob qu
iiiijᵈ the mark	xˢ	xˢ vjᵈ	xjˢ	xjˢ vjᵈ	xijˢ	xijˢ vjᵈ	xiiijˢ	xiiijˢ vjᵈ
iiiijᵈ ob the mark	xjˢ iiijᵈ	xjˢ ixᵈ ob qu	xijˢ iiijᵈ ob	xijˢ xjᵈ qu	xiiijˢ vjᵈ	xiiiijˢ ob qu	xiiiijˢ vijᵈ ob	xvˢ ijᵈ qu
vᵈ the marke	xijˢ vjᵈ	xiiijˢ jᵈ ob	xiiijˢ jxᵈ	xiiiijˢ iiijᵈ ob	xvˢ	xvˢ vijᵈ ob	xvjˢ ijᵈ	xvjˢ xᵈ ob
vᵈ ob the mark	xiiijˢ ixᵈ	xiiiijˢ vᵈ qu	xvˢ jᵈ ob	xvˢ ixᵈ ob qu	xvjˢ vjᵈ	xvijˢ ijᵈ qu	xvijˢ xᵈ ob	xviiij vjᵈ ob qu

The Charge of the stannary court.

Good men you shall understand that we are ass=
embled heer this day for a good and godly pur=
pose that is to minister justice as much to say I with
5   you & you with me may indevour with all our pow=
ers to put down vice and to extoll vertue allways
to be brief in effect is comprehendid in this
word Justicia which by Ethnicks is this defyned
Justicia est virtus tribueus vincuiq' qu'd
10   *suu' est* signifying as much as to restore every
man to his proper right. Now yf Panyms and
Cicero & the learned Romaines which divers others
having no hope of salvacon had such a remors
unto iustice that they greatly extolled & wrote
15   very largely in the praise thereof, what should
we christians then do? Needs must we
ernestly imbrace justice according to the
saying of our blessed saviour & master Christ, *q'd*
Cusaris est date Cilsan let every man have his
20   right & for that cause this court is called the lete
court as much as to say as *dies lutin*, a joyfull day
wherein we may rejoyce when vices are so sup=
pressed & vertues so inhansed that every man may
quietly enjoy that thing that is his. Now the reformac=
25   cion of enormities & offences must needs be
brought to passe by matter of record where
unto you upon your othes do your endevour, there
fore first you good men that are sworne you
shall enquire of all comon bakers among you
30   that mak unholsome bread for mans bodye and
kepe not thessise of them shall ye do us to weete.
Also of all brewers & tapsters that brew & kep not the
assise & sell by cups dishes bolles & by measures
unsealed you shall do us to weet.

Also for your footfates quartes & measurs whether
any tynner use doble measures that is to say a great
measure to buy with & a small measure to sell
with, or useth deceipt amongst the Quenes leige
5   people do us to weet. Also of all such persons
as have measures to meet tyn with all which now
not brought them hither at this law court to be
assured of such shall ye enquire & do us to weet
Also yf there be any wayes lanes or pathes straytid
10   stopt or turned out of his right course into a
wrong course to the anoyance of the Quenes
leige people by occasion of myne pits shafts
hatches or tynworkes & by the maker thereof
not repayred & amended of such offendors you
15   shall enquire & do us to weet.

Also you shall enquire yf any tynner or tyners
have stolne any tyn & their receiters so that the
Lord Wardens officers may sease in the same tyn
so stolne to the use of the Quenes Majestie.

20   Also of all strayers coming wthin the viij tuthings
of this stannary court of Blackmoor of horses,
sheep, swyne, or any other kind of beasts which have
bin there the space of a yeere & not challenged
& the Queen's Majestie not answered thereof you shall
25   enquire & do us to weet.

Also yf there be any amongst you that have kept
black tyn unblowen after the feast of St Mi=
chaell tharchangle where the tyn is how much
it is & who is the owner thereof of all this you
30   shall advertise the court --------- & do us to weet.

Also you shall enquire of all corrupt mettall
of tyn & makers & blowers thereof which have
made the tyn & not set thaccustomed letter upon
the same, that is to say hard tyn not having this
35   letter H. Sinder tyn not having this letter S.

Pyllyon tyn this letter P. & Relystian tyn
this letter R. By deceipt where of the marchant
travelers beyond the seas - - - - often tym
stand in great danger besides the great lostes
5   that they have sustayned thereby. more over ye
shall enquire of such as are blowers of whit
tyn & ar not heer at this law day to take their othe
according to the auncient custome for the true
& just executing of their function in that behalfe
10   the names of them which make default you shall
serch out and do us to weet.

Also you shall enquire of the officers of the - - - - -
coynage or of the courts as the baylife tuthinmen
tollers or any other officer whatsoever whether
15   they omit or slack in any thing to do their dutie
& being fownd out you ought likewise present.

Also you shall enquire & presentment make
of all coliers that carry coales to blowing howses
with coale packes that ar not filled with three bu=
20   shels after xxtie gallons the bushell in mea=
sure for so much must they be by the old aun=
cient custome.

Also you shall enquire & do us to weet whether the
keper of the gaole his underkeeper depute or de=
25   puts or any of them do omit to do his or their
duties in negligent keping of their prisoners
as willingly suffering them to escape, the
partie plentiffe not being satisfyed of his debt
or otherwise if the keeper his underkeper or
30   depute take any excessive fees above the
fees ratid in that behalfe of the prisoners that is
to say at the prisoners coming in to the gaole
vjd. and every day being in the gaole & at the
kepers finding iiijd. And every day being at
35   large and at the kepers finding vd.

But if the prisoner remaine in gaole & list
to be at his owne finding then ought he to pay
nothing to the keper untill such time as he list
to be at the kepers fynding then to pay according
5   to the rate.

Also you shall enquire & do us to weet of all such
as do implead any tynners in any forren court
out of the libertie of the stannary for matters
determinable in this court likewise if any tyn=
10   ner implead another in any foren court for
causes here to be tryed betwene them.

Also yf the worker of any tinworke be stopt
or strayted of the corerse of their water to
serve to the comoditie of working of their tyn
15   whereas there custome hath bin to fet their water
by a certaine order as is to them prescribed
in any place & over any ground with out denyall
of any person of the offenders herein you shall
enquire & do us to weet accordingly.

20   Also you shall enquire & do us to weet of any
tynner or spalier that fetteth a warrant or
supersede as of the peace against any tinner
or spalier except it be only with the warden
or his depute.

25   Also you shall enquire & do us to weet of thes
offendors that is to say if any person or persons enter
into any tinwork with force or violently with
power take away any tyn out of any tinworke.

Also you shall enquire if any person or persons
30   geve or promis any tynworke or part of any tin=
worke that is in variance betwene partie & partie
to any gentleman Juror or to any other to thin=
tent to beare him in the tryall of the title there
of, of thes you shall enquire & do us to weet.

35   Also you you shall inquire & do us to weete
of the names of all thes tynners or spaliers.

Which do or will refuse to pay any such reaso=
nable sume as shalbe assessed upon them to be
paid toward our princes service, the confirma=
con of the Charter or toward any other ne=

5   cessary cause for the comon welth of the
stannaries.

Also yf any person or persons have disseised or
brought out of possession any tynner of any
tynworke or of any part of a tynwork which he

10   hath had in his possession by the space of one
yeere & a day peaceably except it be only by
order of laws, of the offenders there of you shall
enquire and do to weet. Also you shall
enquire of any such person or persons that sell and

15   deliver any white tyn before tyme it is coyned
whereby the Queens majestie shall lose her coynage
& dutie to her grace apertayning.

Now to speak of appellacons to be usid by se=
verall degrees this is the order that hath bin decreed

20   by the most honorable counseile, that if any tinner
be wronged, first he ought to complaine to the
steward of the court & if he being fownd parciall
do him no justice, then let him complaine to the
underwarden, & if he wil not minister to him justice

25   then let him complaine to the cheife warden & if
he there can obtaine no justice let him then
complaine to the princes counsaile, if you
have known any that have broken this godly de=
cree you shall of such offenders do us to weet.

30   Also you shall enquire if that any steward
maior bayliffe or any other officer take any
tollage toll stallage or tolsill in any faires
or markets of any tinner or tynners in
townes portes

Fayres and market of their owne proper
goods. Also if the bayliffe under bayliffe or any
speciall baylife being auctorised by the court
to arest any by vertue of his write or warrant
5   to him directid take more then vjd. for his
arest for such offendour you shall enquire &
do us to weet. And whereas divers tynners
in working of their streame workes with floods
hath conveid & caried the gravell & robble
10   from the said workes to the great rivers & so
from thence with the streame driven them
to the Havens of Plymouth Tynmouth Dart=
mouth ffalmouth and ffoy to the great
hinderance of the havens. So far forth that is
15   for the river of ffowey yt hath bin reportid before
this tyme that the great boates have past up
under Lostwithiall bridge as far up as directly
under the castle of Restormell, where the place
may be seene unto this day as men report that
20   fishermen have moared their boats unto,
whereas now by reason that the tynners do
streame the tayles of their workes directly
into the great river which having his course
towards Lostithiall & Fowey, waters bring=
25   eth with them the rubble garde & sandes so
much quirting up the rivers that small boats &
barges cannot now come but litle more then
halfe the way that it hath used in tymes past:
yet because the Lord of Loughborough late war=
30   den of the stannaries tendering the preservacon
of the havens at a Court holden at Tavistoke
for the tynners of Cornwall in the xiijth yeer
of the Quenes majesties Raigne by advise of aun=
cient customers of the iiij stannaries being
35   there impanelled took order that the ordinance
& statute which they there made should be read

By the steward of every of the said fower
Courts of the stannaries to the Jurats sworn
upon every law day which if any of the stewards should
omit to do & negligently refuse the reading
5   thereof he shall incurr the penalltie of v li
to be levied by *fieri facias* to the use of the
Quenes majeste, therefore in the reading thereof
to you I shall do my dutie & exonerate me
of the penaltie thereof.

10   The Copie of the Ordinance of
the court holden at Tavistoke for
the stannaries of Cornwall.

At the Court holden for the stannary of Corn=
wall at Tavistoke in the Countie of Devon
15   the xxvijth day of August in the xiiijth
yeer of the Raigne of our soveraigne
lady Elyzabeth by the grace of god Quene
of England ffrance & Ireland defendour
of the faith etc. Before the right honorable
20   Lord Edward Hastings of the right honorable
order of the garter knight Lord Hastings
of Loughborough & high warden of the
said stannarie of Cornwall & other the Queen's
majesty's Comissioners there yt is enactid.
25   ffor whereas *it is enacted* for the better
preservacon & maintenance of the havens
& ports of Plymouth ffalmouth & ffowey
there have bin heretofore two sundry statuts
& acts in the high court of Parlyament
30   at Westminster whereof the one in the xxijth yere
& the other in the xxvijth yeer of the Raigne
of the late King of famous memory king
Henry the eight were ordayned and made
In which said statutes it hath

Byn by great pollycie ordayned & devised
that no person or persons from and after the end of
the said parlyament should laboure or work in any
maner tynworks called streame works
5   within the said Cownties of Devon or Cornwall
nigh to any of the fresh water rivers there or
low places descending or having course to the
forsaid havens & ports or any of them nor should
labour dig or washe any tyn in any of the said
10   tynworkes called streame works unles the
diggar owner or washer did make suffici=
ent hatches or tyes in the end of the buddls
& cordes & therein put or lay or cause to be put
& laid all their said stones gravell & rubbell
15   digged about the serching fynding & washing
the said tyn there to be wholy and surely kept
by the said hatches & tyes out and from the
aforsaid freshe rivers upon certain paines
mentioned in the severall estatuts & further
20   as in the same more at large is contayned which
said estatutes for that they not being put in due
execution have not brought such redresse of
the annoysance of the said portes & havens as
thereby was ment & hath bin lookid for. And to
25   the end that the contents of the forsaid severall
estatutes & the mischeifes therein declared may
the better hereafter be reformed: It is farthr
enactid over & besides the penalties & provisons
already ordayned in the said two severall esta=
30   tuts that if upon any bill plaint or informacon
made or exhibited in any of the courts of the
stannarye in the forsaid Countie of Cornwall
against any person or persons for any offence don
contrary to the provision of the said estatuts
35   or either of them. And that the person or persons
so offending be there of duly convictid

Either by verdict of xij men or moe by his or
their owne confession or by any other lawfull
wayes or meanes that the partie or parties so con=
victed for the first offence shall forfait and
5   incur the penaltie of xl markes to be levied
of his goodes & cattals by *fieri facias* as other
penalties & forfeitures ar accustomed to be
levied, the one halfe to be to our Soveraigne
Lady the Quenes majestie her heires & successors
10   thother halfe to the partie that will sue for the same
by bill plaint or informacon etc. And if the
partie so offending do estsoones offend & be
thereof convictid as aforesaid that then he to lose
al such interest estate & terme as he hath in the
15   said workes either in his owne right or in the
right of his wife during his naturall life
the moytie of which said tynworke to be to our
said Soveraigne lady the Quenes majestie and
the other moytie to him that will sue for the same in
20   any of the said stannary courts by bill plaint
or informacon. In which sute no protection ess=
yne or wager of law to be allowed for the de=
fendant. And if the partie or parties so offending
and thereof convictid as aforsaid be not able
25   to pay and satisfye the penaltie of xl
markes aforesaid that then the said partie or
parties shalbe committid to the prison of Lost=
withiell there to have the imprisonment of
one yere without bayle or maineprise. And
30   be hit also farther enactid that if the steward
of the said stannary courts of Cornwall
for the tyme being do not at ech law day to
be holden within the said stannary geve this or=
dinance & statute to the jury of the same court
35   that then the said steward shall for his
            negligens incur the penal=
                  tie.

of v li. for ech time so offending to be lyvied
by *fieri facias* to the use of our Soveraigne
lady the Quenes majestie her heires & successors
and for the better preservacon of the havens
5   aforsaid. Be it further enactid that it shalbe law=
full for any person or persons from henceforthe
working in any hatchworkes or streame workes
to convey & carry their rubble gravell and
sand of any such workes into any hatches tyepits
10   myry places & grownes which have bin of aunci=
ent tyme wrought or any other convenient
places aswell within the lymits & bowndes of the
said tynworkes or elswhere so that it be not prejudicall
to the working of any work already pitched & not
15   throughly wrought unto the shelfe. And it shal=
not be lawfull for any person or persons hereafter
to dig or work for tyn in any streame worke
within three score foot to the maine or great
fresh river comonly called by the names of
20   ffowey river Tamer & other great rivers
going to ffalmouth, Plymouth & fowey runing
or discending unto any of the havens aforsaid
nor shall worke any hatchworke within xxiiij te
foote of any the rivers aforsaid. And that all &
25   every person & persons working in the said
hatchworke shall make & provide such strength
of places stayes so that the force of any of the
aforsaid rivers at the flood or overflowing
of any of them do not carry away any abu=
30   dance of gravell rubble or sand in the noy=
sance or hurt of any of the havens above spe=
cified upon paine of such fine & penaltie as
shalbe asseised for the said offence by the lord
warden or his underwarden in that behalf
35   provided alwaies that no person or persons shall
incurr the danger and penaltie -------------

Off any of the statutes made at this present
great court before publicacon of the ffects of the
same at every of the iiij stannary courts:

5   The appropriate publication has been made in these premises in full
     stannary court of Foymoor at Lantrees on 30th
     day of the month of August in the 13th year of our Lady Elizabeth,
     Queen, in the tinners' province.

              Written under which in his own hand
                        Thomas Bere

10   The appropriate publication in these premises in full court at
     Lostwithiel in the stannary of Blackmoor the 8th day
     of the month of October in the 14th year of the reign of Lady
     Elizabeth, in the tinners province, written under which
     in his own hand. William Kendall.

15   At the making of this act there
              was at Tavistoke in Devon
              for ffoymoor

     Thomas Spoor gentleman Thomas Bere gentleman
     Robert Benny Thomas Collins Stephen Lampen
20   and William Doyngell

              ffor Blackmoor.

     William Kendall gentleman John Launce Richard
     Coryn John Tresulian alias Kerne Mark
     Hawkyn And Richard Nanconan

25   ffor Triwarnhaile.

     John Pomery alias Robert James Drew of Guin=
     nap and John Polperra.

              ffor Penwith and Kirriar.

     John Trounsen Alexander Penhellick
30   and John Chigwyn.

              An exposition made upon the charter
              of tynners.

Lines 4-14 translated from the Latin.

In the yeer of our lord god 1375 being the
fiffteth yere of king Edward the third a parlia=
ment was holden at Westminster whereat greate
complaints of extorcion & cruell dealings were
5 laid to the charge of the officers & rulers of
the said stannary courts. the prince at that tyme
ten yeres of age and Duke of Cornwall
was afterwards crowned king of this noble
Realme of England by the name of king Ri=
10 chard the second. At which parlyament the Charter
of tynners was sharply perused over by the kings
Counsell and by the lords so far forthe that there
was at that instant an exposition made out to
declare playnly the meaning of the darkest clauses
15 of the said charter somewhat straiting the liber=
ties of tynners which afterwards in the 51 yeer
of this kings Raigne was Revoked againe by
the princes Counsell. This exposition I have
thought very necessary to be annexed here=
20 unto grantid out by king Edward the third.

The Copie of the exposion

Edward, by the Grace of God King of England and France, Lord
of Ireland, to the warden of the stannary in the county of Cornwall
who is or for a time was, Greetings. Since
25 the Lord Edward, once King of England our grandfather through
his charter which we have confirmed for the commendation
of the stannaries in the county aforesaid
to the peace and use of his tinners
he conceded to them for himself and his heirs
30 that all tinners aforesaid working
in those stannaries that were within his domain
whilst they are working in those same stannaries are free
and quit of the pleas of bondmen and of all
pleas at the court of him and his heirs

Line 22-34 translated from the Latin.

touching anything whatsoever And that his warden
of the aforesaid stannary or his lieutenant will hold
every plea between tinners aforesaid arising
and between them and any outsiders for every
5   trespass quarrel and contract in places
in which they are working within the aforesaid stannary
customarily arising he also conceded to the same
tinners that they might dig for tin and turves to
find tin wherever it is on his lands moors and wastes
10   and other places whatsoever in the aforesaid county just as by
inspection of the rolls of our chancery it is clear And now
then we judge because the commons and poor men
of the said county by their petition in our present
parliament exhibited to us beg that
15   since you and the aforesaid tinners by the charter aforesaid less
to provide knowledge and more to extract
oppressions and burdens from them and other our subjects
and lest you might make to break the soil and still
may not care to stop we wish on behalf of the oppressed their
20   improvement and quiet to explain all the various doubtful and obscure
words in the aforesaid charter completely fully
and aptly. We, noticing the ambiguity
and singular detriments and that our people
are pressed upon so we are held to abolish by the assent and
25   advice of our prelates earls barons
and other our nobles and magnates in
Parliament assisting us, we wish we declare
we determine and intend for our heirs that
these words above expressed under which and
30   as are following are taken and are understood, viz,
they work in their same stannaries and while
they are working in those same tinworks they must understand
clearly in the works in which they are working

This page translated from Latin.

Gateway from Duchy Palace to Fowey River Quay.   Photograph *Cornwall Archaeological Unit Collection*

and labouring as far as it applies in those tinworks
without fraud and artifice and not for others nor elsewhere working.
And that article that the warden aforesaid
or his lieutenant may hold pleas arising between
5   tinners aforesaid and also between
them and other outsiders for all trespasses
quarrels and contracts made in places
in which they work within the stannary similarly
arising extends to sue in the jurisdiction with
10 the force of words in the charter aforesaid, viz, in
places where these works are worked and not elsewhere
nor another way and so to you in the district in which we can
make judgements we order that from these
extortions oppressions and burdens
15 on our people in the said county moreover applying
to tinners desisting of the aforesaid judgement
on the understanding of the said charter and we wish
that our declaration and decision
as above, by the king made reasonably and
20 fairly, that our people as abovesaid against
the strength force and effect of our words desire
declaration and intention, not be molested
in this or burdened, or to be molested or
to be burdened whatsoever. Written by me
25 at Westminster on the sixth day of July in the fiftieth year
of our reign in England (our true reign)
and the thirty-sixth in France.

One Tynner impledith another
for the entering violently upon
30 his worke.

J.B. seeks against T.S. in a plea of trespass and
therefore the same plaintiff through T.D. his attorney
seeks that the said defendant on 10th
day of May in the 34th year of Henry VIII, by force
35 and arms namely onto one tinwork

Apart from lines 28-30 entire page translated from Latin.

of the man, called a dole of tin next to one
called of 28 doles in P., he entered
and has worked there for black tin and black
tin was then and there found and worked, viz
5   16 feet of black tin to the value of
16s. a foot, he took and carried away as the trespass
aforesaid, the length of which working of black tin
aforesaid was from the said 10th day of May in the 34th year
of our said lord King, until the day of impeachment
10   committed for this dispute, viz, 3rd day of August
in the year aforesaid, for diverse days and weeks continuing
And other things, etc, to the detriment of this
plaintiff from which he says that he has been damaged
and has damage to the value of £40
15   and so he produces suit.

        A Tynner impleded for
        working in severall lands.

J.B. seeks against T.S. in a plea of trespass,
and therefore the same plaintiff, through P.R. his attorney,
20   seeks that since the said defendant on 10th
day of May in the 34th year of King Henry VIII by force and arms
viz, etc, on separate land within the close
of the said plaintiff being at L.(name of place)
in one close there called M. within, etc, he entered
25   and there he bounded and limited a tinwork
within the plaintiff's several land
there, without said licence, where he dug for
black tin and has worked as a trespasser aforesaid,
now he seeks it as a working in the plaintiff's several land aforesaid,
30   from the aforesaid 10th day of May until, etc.

        The forme of a bill of indictment
        for impleding tynners in a foren
        court.

Apart from lines 16,17,31,32,33 entire page translated from Latin.

It is required for the lady Queen when through diverse charters
made and conceded through diverse kings of England and
our ancestors of the Duchess our lady Queen now, etc, And through
the same
lady Queen ratified and confirmed to her tinners
5   in her Duchy of Cornwall, that all tinners of the
aforesaid Duchy of Cornwall working in the County of Cornwall
in stannaries that are in the domain of the lady Queen or of others
in the Duchy aforesaid, while they are working in the same stannary
are free and quit of the pleas of bondmen and of all
10   pleas and quarrels in the court of our lady Queen and her heirs
whatsoever touching therefore that they do not answer
in the presence of any judges or ministers
of the said our lady Queen for any plea or quarrel
within the aforesaid stannary arising except
15   in the presence of the warden of the stannary of the lady Queen
in her Duchy aforesaid, except for plea of land, life and limb.
And therefore S.G. lately of T. in county aforesaid, gent,
in charter aforesaid for very little weighing
and considering the stannary of the lady Queen in her Duchy
20   aforesaid contrary to the tenor of the charter aforesaid, there
we concede to them
rightly to proceed to Bodmin in the county
aforesaid on the 10th day of May in the year, etc, in the presence
of John C. and other judges of the lady Queen, keepers of the peace
of the county, aforesaid, assigned to prosecute
25   diverse bills, pleas and quarrels against
R.R., T.S. and others, worthy of faith and workers
of tin, in the county aforesaid, and for diverse things and
matters in the presence of the warden of the stannary and not
otherwise determining in contempt of the said lady Queen and
30   to the serious detriment of the working of tin in the county
aforesaid and not in evil and pernicious example of others
in any such case of delinquency except upon this more speedy
remedy it be applied opportunely, etc, and
against, etc.

35   One tynner impleadeth another
            for forme of a Tynworke.

Apart from lines 35,36 the whole page translated from Latin.

P.B. is summoned to reply to J.C. for the plea that
he render to him 3s.4d. which he owes him and unjustly
keeps as he says, And therefore the same plaintiff in his own
person says that when he, on the 8th day of October,
5   in the year of the reign, etc, at T. within, etc, handed over and
demised to the same Peter for one tinwork of his
called a dole of a tinwork in C. to have,
work and occupy to the same Peter from the aforesaid 8th
day of October in the year aforesaid, until the feast of St Michael
10   the Archangel then next following, Rendering and
paying therefore to the same John C. and his assigns
3s.4d. for the farm of his tinworks
aforesaid, at the aforesaid feast of St Michael the Archangel by
virtue of which lease the aforesaid P.B. his aforesaid tinwork
15   from the aforesaid 8th day of October
in the year above written, up to the feast of St Michael the
Archangel then next following, has had, worked and
occupied and the aforesaid 3s.4d. as rent and
farm aforesaid, for that time to the same John C.
20   from the above arising, has not been paid, for which action increases
to the same John C. to demand and have from the aforesaid
P.B. the 3s.4d. However, the same
P.B. is allowed more time to find the rent aforesaid, 3s.4d. to
               the same
J.C., he does not render meantime. But the paying of the same
25   he denied and still denies from which
he has been damaged and has damage to the value
of 2s. and therefore he produces suit.

          The answere of a foryner
          in the stannary court.

30   And the aforesaid A. in his own person comes and says, that
       this court does not have jurisdiction to hold a plea on this
matter under discussion aforesaid, as specified, because he says that

Apart from lines 28,29 whole page translated from Latin.

He is not nor ever was a tinner or worker
in tin in the demesne land of the lady Queen or
any other person, or matter in the said discussion
is not contained in any tinwork nor touching tin
5   nor pertaining from which, thus, he seeks judgement whether this
court wishes him to speak further, or thus he seeks judgement
whether this court has jurisdiction to hold
a plea, etc.

10   The forme of a declaracon against
          tynners streaming the tayles of their
          workes into the fresh rivers contrary to
          the statute and ordinance.

Robert T. & M.N. were summoned to reply to W.B.
who both for the Lady Queen and for seisin causes
15   this plea, that they render to him 20 of lawful money
of England, that they owe to the Lady Queen and the aforesaid W.B.
and unjstly keep from him by a scheme attempted against the form
of statute in parliament of the Lord King Henry VIIIth
lately King of England, etc, and much to be feared,
20   by the Lady Queen now Elizabeth, by the Grace of God, etc, at
Westminster in the 27th year of her reign, therefore those who work
or labour or cause to be worked or laboured
in any tinworks called 'streame
workes' within the counties of Devon and Cornwall near
25   standing waters, whether lower or flat places,
having courses to the ports of Plymouth Tynmouth
Falmouth and Fowey determined and proved, etc, And so the same
W.B. who both for the Lady Queen and for himself, causes
in his own person and says that since in a statute of parliament
30   aforesaid of Lord King Henry VIIIth at Westminster
on the day in the 27th year of his reign above written by authority
of the same parliament amongst others enacted thus, that
no person whatsoever shall work or labour in
any tinworks called 'stream workes' within
35   the counties of Devon and Cornwall near any standing
waters, whether any lower or flat places

Apart from lines 9-12 whole page translated from Latin.

that have course to the ports of Plymouth, Teignmouth,
Dartmouth, Falmouth and Fowey or to any
port of these, nor work the aforesaid and wash any
tin in any tinworks called
5 'streame workes' unless they make sufficient sumps
and ponds in the end of the buddles and cords
called in English 'cordes' and there to put up all
stones and sand dug for banking of the tin aforesaid
and keeping it there safe and sound from the aforesaid
10 fresh rivers and waters, so that none of the aforesaid with
stone and sand dug around the banking
of the tin aforesaid any flushing whatsoever of pits and
sumps through rain and flood water be carried out
to any aforesaid port under penalty of forfeiture
15 as often as such occurs, etc, at whatever time,
of 20 of which one half is for the said
Lady Queen and the other half of that is for the same
that has wished to prosecute through the original writ, bill or
plaint as owed, or through a deposition in any
20 court of the said Lady Queen to which action and
suit no pledging at law be admitted for the defendant
nor any excuse or protection be allocated
just as is contained in the statute aforesaid more fully
yet R.T. and M.N. by small statute aforesaid hanging
25 and the penalty of the same statute nothing fearing
or dreading, 20th April in the 16th year of the reign
of the said Lady Queen Elizabeth, by the Grace of God, etc,
after the commencement of the act aforesaid at Lanharne
Moor, within the jurisdiction
30 of this court in that tinwork called
Lanharne Moor in the said county of Cornwall within,
etc, lying near the water or river there
having its course to the port of Fowey for
black tin they have laboured and have been working
35 not having sufficient sumps

Entire page translated from Latin.

and pits in the ends of the buddles and cords there to
keep safe and secure the stones and sand
dug for the enclosing of tin from the aforesaid remaining
sand having its course to the port of Fowey
5   as near the form of the aforesaid statute that the action increased
to the same W.B. to demand and to have from the aforesaid
defendant for the said Lady our Queen and for himself
that 20 to the same that R.T. and M.N.
are more often required to pay that 20 to the same W.B.
10   for the said Lady Queen and for himself not
paying up anything but to those thay have claimed not to pay to
and still claim not to, whence the same
W.B. says that it has deteriorated and that he has damage to
the value of 10 and so he has a suit to his aforesaid
15   Lady Queen and for himself And the foresaid R.T. and M.N.
through W.C. their attorney come and defend,
etc, And verification remaining for this plea still
says that he himself has made a dam at the end of the cords
and buddles sufficiently secure to protect
20   and guard against other problems whatever they might be to the
detriment of the port of Fowey in manner and form as
in the statute demands, and so from this he seeks a
judgement if the aforesaid Lady Queen and the said W.B.
must continue to have their action aforesaid
25   against them, etc.

        The reply of W.B. for the Lady Queen
        and for himself.

On that day came the said W.B. both for the said Lady
Queen and for himself, and he says that he for the said
           plea against the said
30   R.T.,etc, made in manner and form aforesaid, believes that
           it be not necessary
nor through the law of this land to be forced to reply
and so with this as sufficient defence in this part arising, he seeks
judgement and that the owed 20 with his damages
on the occasion of the detention owed to him aforesaid is awarded

35   Causes are (?)

Entire page translated from Latin.

The defendant is charged for working in Lawharne
Moore having no sufficient hatches &
tyes in the end of his buddles & cordes etc
for answere whereunto he saith that he made sufficient
5   saffegard in the end of his buddles & cordes
to kepe the gard & other ylles which should
hinder the port of ffoy & doth not alleage that
he made it sufficient in the end of all the
buddels etc. Also he doth not alleage that it was
10   so at the xjth day of May *Ano supdict* which
ought to have bin certen, for albeit it were
amended after, yet the cause of accon
once geven the offence is not thereby dischar=
ged so that his issue should have bin that he himself, the aforesaid
15   defendant on the said 11th day of May in the year aforesaid has
a fine of all buddles and cords, etc, sufficient
hatches and wells to draw from, etc,
in the form, etc, thus, that no piece of stone
or sand he digs there through, etc, he has drawn up, etc,
20   for defect(? defence),etc, Wherefore the said W.B. prayeth
Judgement for the Quene & himselfe for
the debt damages & costs of sute etc.

        Off two divers bownds upon one
        tynworke the one before the worke was
25   vacant and the other afterward.

In this present 1586 there chansed varience
to fall betwene coopartners of one tynwork
so that the one company went secretly about
to have there work new bownded & to bring
30   it into such strangers hands as they might
order according to their will & pleasure
that whereas their workings before time
xvij or xviij doles they would then bring
yt to halfe company by which he meanes they
35   might have the more right them selfes

Lines 14-20. Mostly Latin translated into English.

To there owne use but in the name of theire
child, brother or dear freind for if that one
old owner be knowen to be an owner with the
new pitches he being so once knowen bringith
5   in with him all the whole company of his fellows
therefore they made their new pitchers privy that
the day of bownding was in the xxth day of
Septembre last past which day they would let
slip bringing their tynwork vacant for want
10   of reneuing. this next company attending di=
ligently upon the said xxth day of Septembre
came & new bownded the tynwork the vary same
day being the old owners very day of bonding
whereas indeed the yere was passed but that
15   was the very day for tynners by their cusome
have alwayes a yere & a day which day followeth
after the yeer. And by theis meanes the new
Company made their new pitch one day before
their work was void. A subtile tynner espying
20   out this fault that the bownes of the new company
were in one day before the worke was vacant
cometh the morrow or the next morrow after
that & casteth upon hit the second pair of bonds
at which day the work was void in very deed &
25   so by that meanes gote the worke into his handes
from the old owners & also the other pitchers by
reason that their pitch was before the worke was
vacant. this the coopartners of the old owners
deceaved their fellowes and them selves &
30   the new bownders left the worke likewise that
title was tryed at a speciall court holden
for Blackmoor in the viijt. day of Aprill last
viz Ao. 1586.

35   Off a tynwork bownded by two severall
Companyes the first company not entring
the proclamacon into the court books and the
last having his proclamation entred.

The like quarrle but after another sort chan=
sed this present yeer. Certaine owners of one
auncient tynwork whether negligently or
willingly (I know not) suffered certaine tails
5   to come into their worke above the space of one
yeer & a day & within that space never turned them
out as it was geven in evidence which is a plane
forfait of a tynworke which forfait being a espied
by other tynners they new bownd the same
10   they make two defaults more the one is that
they bownded the tynworke & the tye with one
peare of bownds which as tynners
say they may not do by the custome for they should
have set one pear of bownds upon the tynwork
15   & another payre upon the tye, another fault
there was for that they entred not their proclama=
con into the court bookes. theis defaults with
others more was espied out by a tinner which
came & cut the second new bownds upon the said
20   tynworke entring his ploclamacon upon
the court books in the next court then insu=
ing & so proceeding orderly then cometh the former
bownders & forbiddeth this proclamacon entring
there accon of trespas against the latter bow=
25   nders, as the order is presupposing that the said
latter bownders such a day and tyme had
entred with force uppon their peaceable pos=
session of their tynwork presupposing damages
of a C li. the defendant by protestacon saith that neither
30   the said former bownders had any possession
in the said work neither yet any proclamacon
in Court but for answere not guiltye this trial
coming to issue at a speciall court holden
upon the same worke the Jury impanelled
35   and sworne passed with the latter bownder

Of the said Tynwork as well for that they had
made but one pear of bownds about the tye &
the tynworke & for that they had entred no proclama=
tion in court as also for other defaults but
5   cheifly because they had not entred their pro=
clamacon in court theire Counsall alleged
by way of plea that it was at theire election
whither they would enter their proclamacon in
court or not which was spoken by the
10   Counseller as I suppose for no other purpose
but that he must say somewhat for his fee. ffor in
very deed I have knowen that one William Beere
Esquire being steward of the stannary court
under the Lord Russle chefe warden of the stanary
15   by the most noble King Henry the eight his
tyme that when a proclamacon hath bin entred
in Court he hath proceeded calling the same pro=
clamacion at three severall courts then
next ensuing and at the last court if no man
20   came to forbid the proclamacon then hath he en=
tred for Judgement upon the proclamacion
being so required by the party pl(?) taking iiijd. for
his fee: *"Gaudeat opus stannar' p'd,"* etc. And
upon the same an Injunction granted at the
25   request of the bownder directed to the baylif
of the court to avoid the old owners from their
possession & to put the new in possession of theire
work. So now among thes 3 claymers this contro=
versie yet remayneth undiscussed as the saying is
30   *"Causidici certat et adhuc subjudice liz est."* the old
owners have yet unto this tyme this work in possession
& have delyvred tyn upon the same work making
8 or 9 foot to a dole which old owners being in possess=
ion of the worke should have denyed the proclamacon
35   & none other, this matter in very deed is like
to come before the vice warden before they can
agree upon yt.

The Contents of this booke.

33. How the Marchant taking lost in sale of
corrupt tyn may be answered of his losts.

33. That the blower is most blameworthy of
corrupt tyn without his letters H.S. or p. etc.
What measures they have to meat theire
tynne within Blackmoor. 35.

35. How the tynners of Blackmoor meat their tynne,

Divers masters delyvering out their mony upon
white or black tyn to the spalier which shall
have the tynne. 37.

Off coliers and Cole cariers. 37

How much the Coale pack ought to be. 38.

38. Of Aresting tyn in strife betwene party & party.

What remedy the owner of the blowing house
hath for tyn which is blowne to his howse the
Cawle and charges not paid for. 39.

The Custome yf the toller keep not his hower
to delyver the blacke tyn. 39.

Off the fees of the gaole. 40.

That the spalier ought not to be impleaded
for working. 41.

No black tyn ought to remaine unblowne
after Michelmas. 41.

No Tynner for tynmatter ought to assent
to the tryall of the same in a forren court. 41.

41. The answere of a tyner in a forren court.

One tynner ought not to implead another
out of the tyn court. 42.

Of the stannary of ffoymoore & of
their measures to meat theire tyn.

In perusing over that which I have written here be=
fore I can fynd but very small diversitie in
5   Customes & usages betwene the stannaryes of
Blackmoor & ffoymoor as far as I can yet
understand of the wise men of that stannary with
whom I had some conference to that intent that I
would attaine to some knoledge saving only in
10   theire tyn measures & in the meating of their
tyn for as I have writen before pagina 35.

Blackmoor tynners meat their tyn with two
measures that is the foot fate & the quart fate with
as light measure as can be, their foot fate con=
15   tayneth two gallons & a pottle wine measure
their quart fate contayneth one pottle & a pynt
so that of theis measures the tynners hold opinion
that eight foot being of the best streame worke tyn
& well purifyed at the most will make 250
20   pownds of white tyn which they accompt to be
a quarter pece of white tyn for that fewer of thes
peeces make a thousand and the charges of
the blowing discharged beside that is every three
foot & one quart or somwhat lesse of their mea=
25   sure meat after the lightest sort will make a
hundred of white tyn. Now then let us bring
their light measure to pack measure for as I
wrote before pagina. 35. the foot fate after
their measure or meating will hold one quart
30   more if it were well packed as they use in
ffoweymoor. Now to make it pack measure
whereas 3 foot & one quart light met will
make one hundred of white tyn upon every
foot abate one quart & of the quart abate one
35   quarter of a quart so have you brought
their light measure to Daye measure then
two foot & three quarters of a
        quart & somwhat lesse

Will make one hundred of white tyn by the mea=
sures of Blackmore being packt which they co=
monly call Day measure. So now you may com=
pare ffoymoor measures & meating with theris (theirs).
5   The tynners in ffoymoore meat their tyn at
their washes by the gallon packing of their
measures as fast & hard as possible may be which the buy=
er him self shalbe permitted to do if he list or any
other at his appointment. ffower of thes
10   gallons (as they say) maketh a foot of theire me=
asure, then their measure which they call the
gallon doth containe five wine quarts & a pynt
then fower of the gallons packt wth mine tyn
well dressed & purified will make one hundred
15   of white tyn. And .3. gallons & one halfe gal=
lon of theire streame worke tyn or moor tyn
being well clensed washed & purifyed will
make one hundred of whit tyn, so in com=
paring the one wth the other you shall find
20   no great oddes betwene them yf any be the
larger of both it is Blackmoor.

            Blackmoor: ii foot pack measure a hundreth
                                iii qartrs of a quart of whit tyn

            ffoweymoor: iii gallones hundreth of
25   pack measure white tyn.
                                one pottle

Bring you .3. gallons & one pottle of ffoy=
moor measure into pynts which is a 37 pints
Do you the like with two foot three quarters
30   of a quart of Blackmoor measure and yt
wilbe 40 pynts, so there is but iii pynts
oddes which is gotten up in the measure of ffoy=
more being very much packed.

            Off myne tyn and moor tynne
            alias streame worke tynne.

As there are two divers sortes of black tyn
so ought they to be diversly dressed & used, the
streame work tyn is such a great graine of
tyn that it is dressed & purified with small char=
5   ges: but for that the myne tyn lyeth in the hard
stone it must be stampt in stamping milles
or grownd in crasing mills & have buddels
made even for the purpose to washe purifie
& separate the waste from the tyn so that to
10   bring it to his profit graine it requireth no
litle labour then because of the lightnes of
the measure thereof the more quantitie of
this tyn goeth to the making of a hundred
of white tyn therefore must this myne tyn
15   have a price according.

        That there was no tyn in vallyes
        & moores before the generall flood
        called Noyes fflood.

I have heard reported that before the generall
20   fflood called Noyes flood there was no
tyn in the moores low grownds & vallyes
but the tyn lay hid in the rocks hills & great
mines so that the strength of the flood brea=
king forth from the high grownd caried
25   with violence the most gloriest fattest
& principall of all the tyn laboring so
far that they never payd untill tyme that they
came unto the low vallyes which ar the very
same workes that we call streame workes
30   hatchworkes & moorworkes.

        How the exposition made in the 50 yere
        of King Edward the 3. Raigne was made
        frustrate in the yeere following.

You had before pagina 78 how that the parliament
holden in the 50 yere of the Raigne of King Ed=
ward the third there was an exposition made
upon the charter of tynners upon greavous
5   complaints made against them which exposition
was to the great decay of the franchises &
liberties of tynners as by the same you may
understand at large in the yere after being
in the yere of our lord 1377 & in the eight
10 day of June being Trynitie sonday prince
Edward called the black prince departid out
of this life which in his tyme was the flower
of Chivalry he was buried at Canturbury
and the king Edward creatid Richard sone
15 of prince Edward Errle of Chester Duke
of Cornwall & prince of Wales. In this 51
yere of the kings raigne upon supplication
made by the said prince Richard & his coun=
sell the said exposition was made frustrat
20 & void as by a copie of the said supplica=
tion hereunto anexed being in frence
preserved & exhibited to the king & his
Counsaile as ye may perceive by the tenor
therof.

25   *Allocacois libert stannar'*
            Ducat Cornub'

        The copie of the supplication made
        by Richard prince of Wales &
        Duke of Cornwall to King Edward.3.

30 Monstre humble fitz Richard prince de
Gales a nostre soigniour Le Roy comet'
La on son signiour & pier monster Ed=
ward Nagaires prince de Gales quedi
eux afforle effoit feaseis & en possession

Line 21. frence=French
Lines 30-34 in 14th century French. Untranslated.

De Estanries de Cornwall et Devonshere
onesq'(?) certan franchises et libert' aptenant
N as(?) ditz estan'ez Ashthun' p' chartre du
roy Ashchun' comen droyt et Ashchun' p'
5   usage et costome uses de toutz tempz de ne
morie memtenois p' peticien sauus p' asth(?)'
de ditz courtez en le parliament tenus aues=
nd darrier ant cest estoit fait declacono'
de la ditz chartre touchant le ditz franchises
10   et liberties et usages samus(?) ceo H sou de seig=
niour et periene(?) null' aut pour le p'tie
de lux ne de ditz Richard d'ne pour le di=
ciez Esteynries estounte appeles ne oyer
ala dit declaracon la gel est trouez et
15   terneroit a graunde dissei son et distr=
uction de ditz estendies et en grande dis=
herison et Dayiage Du ditz Richard en
countre le leye et reason sole ditz Richard
g'el please a nostre seigniour le roye en
20   cet present parliament adnuller le ditz decla=
racon attenda g'ell est estout error nouse=
ment fait cu' de suis est dit et po(?)arceo nostre
seigniour le Roy restitutz le ditz Richard
en possession de ditz franchises liberties
25   et usages p' le maner g'son ditz peir
laime seignior de Esteineres ley ten=
us et uses de tout temps cu' de suis est dit.

In Rotulo p'liamenti de an quin
quayessimo primo Regis Edwardo'
30   *Henrii in allocacoe libert' stanaria*
rum. Ducatse Cornub'.

This act past in 51 yere of the Raigne of King Edward 3. &
in the 21 day of June in that present yere being in
the yere of our Lord god 1377. the noble King Edward
35   the third departid this mortall life.

From line 30 on page 98 to line 27 page 99, the 14th century French of
the Parliamentary Roll has been left untranslated.

The forsaid supplication drawn
and convertid into Englishe.

Most humbly complayneth your sonn Richard
prince of Wales to our lord the king that
5   whereas his lord & father Lord Edward late prince
of Wales whom god hath called to his mercie
was seised & in possession of the stannaries of
Cornwall & Devon together with certaine
franchises & liberties apertayning to the said
10   stannaries some by charter grantid by the
king & some by comon right & some by usage
& custome used out of tyme & memory of men
untill at the parliament holden at Westminster
last before this peticon was made to have
15   an exposition made of the said Charter
touching the said franchises liberties &
usages without that our said lord & father nei=
ther any other in the behalf of him nor
yet in the behalfe of the tynners being
20   called to the hearing of the said declaracon
or exposition the which is fownd & holden
to the great disheriting & damage of the
said Richard & contrary to all law & rea=
son if redresse thereof be not had where
25   uppon the said Richard doth make supplication
that it would please our Soveraigne
lord the king to frustrate & adnull the
said exposition entending verifying &
upholding that the same was erroniouslye
30   made as before is said & there upon that our
Soveraigne lord the king would refer the
said Richard in possession of his said fran=
chises liberties & usages after the maner
that tynners have used of the stannaries in
35   old tyme as before is said.

This is contayned in the parlyament
Roll of the one & feftith yere of King
Edward the third in allowing
the lyberties of the stannaryes of
5   the Duchie of Cornwall.

That there is gold among the tyn.

There is no doubt but if we had amongst our
tyners finers that could fyne purifie & separ=
ate the most precious mettals one from an=
10   other there would as perfyt gold be had out
of our tyn as may be fownd in any contry as
about 36 yere past my fortune was to be present
at a washe of a Tynwork in castle parke by Lo=
stwithiall where at there was a certaine
15   gentleman present whom I could name he ga=
thering out from the heap of tyn certaine
glorious cornes affirmed them to be pure
gold which the tyners permitted him very gently
as they will gentilly suffer any man to doe
20   most chefly if any of liberalitie wilbestow
amongst them but the value of one ijd.
to drink then shall you have them very
diligently to go to their buddels them selfes
& seek out amongst the cornes of tyn which
25   they call Rux the finest & most radianest cornes
& present them to you. In fine amongst other
talke the gentleman shewed a gold ring that he weared
upon his fingar affirming upon his credit
the same ring to be made of certaine gould
30   hoppes that he had gathered among the tyn cornes
at a washe made in a stream worke together with
one ring more which another gentleman had & named
the gentleman so that thes two rings were valued to be
xxvjs.viijd. a peece.

And upon farther talke one ------- David
being there at that present tyme which was a
marchant traveler in partes beyond the seas
reportid that he & one John Vanston another
5   marchant traveler having at Burdiaux
certaine tyn to be sold there cometh to them two
florentines which bought all their tyn in the
overvewing of which tyn they fixed their sight
most cheefly upon two peeces which lay in a place
10   beside the rest upon thes two peeces they had
great & secret conference but what theire
talke was the said David could not gather
because he was altogether ignorant of theire
language, yet suspecting that the said two
15   peeces excelling in goodnes the residue of
the tyn, was had in more estimacon of the
fflorentines then any of the other removed
the said two peeces from thence into a secret
place whereas the said peeces lay, after
20   when the said fflorentines came to receave
their tyn & to make payment for the same they
sought for the said two peeces & finding two
other in their places demanded where they
had bestowed the two peeces lying together in
25   that place, the sellers of the tyn affirmed them
to be the same peeces & not changed but that
could not pacifye them, for in the end after
much broyle the fflorentines confessed that
they would not spare that two peeces for all the
30   residue of the tyn which as I suppose was for no
other purpose els but only for love of the gold
to be fined out of the said tyn. Now then
for as much as we have such profitable casual=
ties to be selectid out from our black tyn
35   other els fined & seperatid from our whit
               tyn

It were a necessary and most profitable art
within this our Realme & contry to retaine
some artificiall finers to be conversant amongst our
workers of tyn which have the art to purifie the
5   gold from the other mettle so theis being pu=
rifyed & brought to perfect gould yet that not with
standing our tyn should have nothing the
lesse price at the hands of the Marchant byers
of white tyn, by thes meanes if we were di=
10   ligent we might happely bring three things
to passe & nothing hurtfull to the sale of our
tyn, thone is, the gould to be convertid to
the Queen's majesties treasures which by our Charter
hath the prerogative thereof; the second is that
15   some Contry man borne amongst us desirous
to learn espieth out not only the art of fyning
but also by that diligent meanes getteth the
knoledge to make the most of our tyn amongst
our selfes. thirdly the comodities that they have
20   in far contryes by our tyn redowneth to the
profyt of our owne Contry, where by our own
contry men becometh most profitable mem=
bers of the comon Welthe of the whole Realm
ffor no doubt the wares that we sell out of our
25   Country is caried into far contryes which wa=
res being artificially wrought marchant tra=
velers bring home to us againe after such
sort that we ar driven to buy our owne wares
being fynely convertid by workmanship
30   at fower tymes dearer hand then we sold
yt. thes things which I have seene & heard
of, I thought yt good to make a note in
brief rehersall thereof referring the credit
of the same to the gentill reader.

How to prove whether black tyn
be well purified or not.

The Marchants that buy the black tyn use to tak
a quantitie out of the heap upon the point of
5   a shovell trying yt with the water from the
point backward to the bredth of the shovell by which means
they shall perceave the waste fleeting from the blacke
tyn, yet a more perfyter way they have then this:
for when they come to a heap of black tyn ready to
10   be delivered they will go to the water & weat their
hands dropping weat & from the water thrust their
weat hands into the tyn or heap of tyn by this
meanes shall they try whether the tyn be well clen=
sed or not for if there by any wast among the tyn
15   the wast cleaveth straight way about theire weate
hands which they will washe into a skowpe of water
were as the garde & wast doth quickly try himselfe &
will abide no water whereas the tyn will abide
at astay. this may ye then note that if in so small
20   quantitie of black tyn there remaine so much
waste then must the wast be great in the whole
heape.

To buy blacke tyn by weight.

They say also that there is great tryall of blacke
25   tyn in the waight of a foot of our principall god
streamework tyn. of our light measure will
waigh 70 pownds which tynne waying so much will
abear right well to have the price after vd. the
marke or better, if the foot way 60 li then 4d.ob.
30   the marke yf 50 li. then iiijd. the marke & so
according to the waight of the foote of black
tyn, farther they have had experience that 2 li. of
black tyn will make one pownd of white tyn, so
that after that rate if whit tyn be worth vd. the pownd
35   then is the black tyn worth 2d.ob. the pownd
therefore the surest way is to buy blacke tyn
by the pownd.

Off the blowing of whit tyn.

Although the attempt of myne may seeme very
presumptuous that I having small experience
& lesse knoledge in making of whit tyn, should
5   take upon me to instruct others & to prescribe ru=
les to the ignorant in that faculty wherby they
might learn to follow the most profitabelest order
in the blowing of their black tyn whereas I
myselfe want a skillfull teacher in that service
10   yet may I very well disclose unto the reader
what lost I have had by my negligence in blo=
wing of white tyn. And likewise on thother
side of circumspect attendance aboute the
blowing thereof I have brought black tyn
15   to yeld whit tyn at the largest, for by negli=
gent forsight of xij foot before this tyme being
light measure after the custome of Blackmoor
I have had scarse one quarter peece of whit
tyn which hath had so ill speed partly by bringing it
20   to be blown when the house hath bin cold partly
by wast that hath bin among the black tyn and
most cheifly by setting confidence in others which wei=
ghed very litle other mens losts for I do remem=
bre a proverb writen in Saphick verses although
25   after the most barbarous sorrt but having
a sent somewhat smelling of good counsell.

If thow willt have they cawses sped
Send forth thy servant true
But if thow wishe it well in deed
30   Send none, thy selfe go thou.

Although I had lerned this lesson before, yet
being negligent I put it not in use, untill
I had to my lost tryed out the profe thereof
upon a certaine tyme I hav gotten together

Upon a certaine tyme I had gotten together
as much black tyn of Blackmoor loose measure
as came to the quantitie of xiijtine foot being som
streame worke tyn & some myne tyn one mingled
5   among another whereas in deed I should have
kept the streame worke tyn & myne tyn a sonder
one from another for the moor tyne that will abide
the strength of the wind & the other canot with out
watering to make this tyn whit I was suter
10   to one of my neighbours being owner of a
blowing house desiring a streame to blow
this tyn, a tyme I had appointid unto me ac=
cording to myne owne desire the howse being
throughly heat & good perfycte state to make
15   white tyn & because I would have my tyn well
purifyed & clensed at the tyme of the blowing
I had presently with me a skillfull tynner at
the buddle place by the blowing house
which with the harder streame of water fleeting
20   through the buddle devided first the greatest
streame worke tyn out by him selfe from the
smaller graine of moor tyn, taking lesser
water running through the buddle separated
the courser moor tyn from the small mine
25   tyn, thirdly abating the water with a soft stre=
ame to bring the small myne tyn to his graine
all being receaved at the britch of the buddle
into a lincloth set there for the purpose
that I would lose no part thereof not so much as
30   the very waste that came thereof where in there
might be some tyn although litle. Now in this
meane tyme was this blowing howse ready in
very good & perfyt estate to receave into his hote
hearth every kind of tyn straight from the
35   washing.

ffirst the greatest streame worke tyn, conse=
quently the small moor tyn, lastly the small myn
tyn & finally the wast. So that the blowing house
had his perfyt kind of heat to work his full ope=
5   racon, every sort of black tyn purifyed with
water according to his kind, the blower like=
wise being very expert in the art of blowing
set the tyn to work after such order as follo=
weth the black tyn was cleane moulten into
10   the hearth & very white tyn appeered in the
flote whereat I marvelling not a litle deman=
ded of the blower where the tyn was become
the blower knowing what I meant by my words
willed me to mistrust nothing but affirmed
15   that the black tyn would prove much better that
did yeld white tyn from the fat sinder which
they call the kirnals then that which yeldeth the
white tyn into the flote which proved to be so in ve=
ry deed: ffor of xiij foot of black tynne
20   I had 408 li. of white which was blowen in one
tyde & three howers: for this is to be notid that
if you make not 300 li. of white tyn in one
tyde which is xij howers or at the worst way
litle lesse, then is there a fault in your black
25   tyn being not wel clensed, or els in the blow=
ers negligence or in the blowing house. Thes
have I writen gentill reader only to thet intent
that if you suppose my doings to be profitable in this
small quantitie of black tyn which I had then
30   may you worke the like in your great abundance
of black tyn although it be to the value of 20
hogsheads for in myne opinion you can never
bestow your time better then to new washe & draw
through the buddle all your black tyn when you bring
35   to the hearth to be made white.

The making of the hearth
of the blowing howse.

I have heard the blowers of tyn report that
there is great consideracon to be had in the blow=
5   ing house in making their hearth when they set
their blowing house to worke. for a blower that is ex=
pert in his occupacon as sone as he cometh into a
blowing house being set to work if he do but once
hear the billowes blowing will decerne what falt
10   there is in the hearth, And concerning the rule
thereof this hath bin the opinion amongst them
selves that if the billowes be two foot in the britche
(in the deepth of the billowes I meane) then must
there be xiiij inches from the hearth eye to the
15   tyn hole whereas the tyn cometh out. for if the
hole be ney to the hearth then will the heat of the
billowes be so nigh that it will quickly consume
away the fore part of the hearth, Now if the billo=
wes be lesse bredth then ten or twelve inches
20   will serve from the hearth eye to the tyn hole
if this be not considered by the blower the maker
of the white tyn may quickly lose xls. or more
in the blowing of his tyn.

Off the meating of black tin in
25   ffoweymoore and Blackmoor.

As I wrote to you before comparing the measures
of foymoor & Blackmoor together. ffirst I
say for Blackmoor, one foot of their black
tyn being the best streame work after their
30   light meating waighing three score & ten pownds
will make xxxv li. of white tyn so that you have a
great quantitie of tin to be blowen together
for that the more good tyn you have the better will
the prove be in the blowing. then if one foot
35   make 35 li. of white tyn ij foot & one half
foot after their light measure will make

lx li. of white tyn that is ten pownds above
one quarter peece which no doubt must be very
good streame work tyn if it do so. then it follo=
with that every three foot of good streame worke tynne
5   so met makith cv li. of white tyn. Now come to
ffoymoor measure as they say 3 gallons & one
pottle of their measure maketh one hundreth
of whit tyn, then is three foot of Blackmoore
measure met loose somewhat better then 3 gallons
10   & one pottle of ffoymoor measure for it maketh
v li. of whit tyn more.

Off the post conages.

The Charter grantid to the tynners doth expres
that all black tyn should be made white & coyned with
15   the Queen's majesty's hamer yerely before the feast of St.Mi=
chaell tharchangle & upon paine of forfiture which
no doubt was a very good order for the price of
tyn when it was diligently kept, but now they
breaking that order after Michelmas coynage
20   worke againe for black tyn, wrought & blowen
after Michelmas which bringeth all out of order
& greatly hindereth the price of tin, the reason
is this as the tyn buyers them selfes have reportid
that when they have bought tyn at Michelmas coy=
25   nage & caried the same tine to be sold at the
market in parties beyond the seas being in possi=
bilitie to have a good price to their tyn, then
sudenly before their prise be throughly made
there cometh other marchants with tyn from the
30   post conage Utterly bringing downe their price
by which meanes if the tyn buyer take so great a
lost then must the sellers at the comom conage
take mor lost for what marchant is he which being
once deceaved by meanes of a post coynage
35   will put confidence againe in the comon coynage
knowing more tyn to come after him to the

Distroying of the sale of his tyn but how this
may be remedied I se no way as long as the
masters which deliver mony before upon the black tyn
to the tyn workers which they them selfes have taken
5   before of the marchant tyn buyers So that the
buyers of the white tyn are owners of the
tyn before tyme that the blacke is other wrought
out of the grownd or els made white.

This bringeth the workers of black tyn in
10   their masters debt that geveth them mony upon their
black tyn & there masters likewise falleth
in debt to the marchant buyers of white tyn
and by that occasion ar they compelled to
work after Michelmas for black tyn to
15   keep touch with their masters & their masters
likewise to kepe touch with the tyn buyers &
yet all this will not serve their turne
to bring them out of debt but to confesse the
plaine veritie the good tynworkes are
20   so greatly decayed in all places that the
poor tynners ar scarse able to pick out
a lyving by that occupacon.

The second Table.

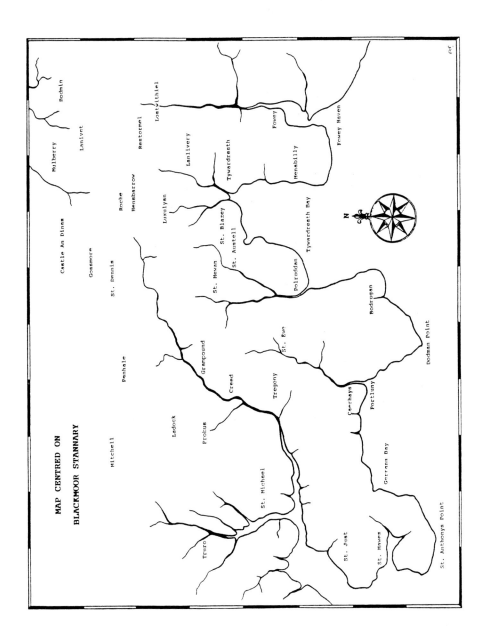

MAP CENTRED ON
BLACKMOOR STANNARY

NOTES & COMMENTS

PAGE 1
Line 6. sercers = searchers.
Line 14. mattox (OE Mattuc). Pickaxe with cutting end instead of point.
Line 14. holme. Old name for holly tree.
Line 22. Spaliard. Tinworker/labourer who stands in for a shareholder in bounds; i.e. in lieu of the absent shareholder's 'spale'.
Line 31. Banishment of Jew by Edward I. George Borlase's 18th century copy of Beare has 15,260 instead of 15,060.
Line 39. xxxii.j th = 33rd.

PAGE 2
Line 4. y̅ = them.
Line 9. obtened = obtained.
Line 15, 22. Sheere/sheer = shire.
Line 25. Ewa = St Ewe.
Line 35. amerced. Fined.
Lines 30, 31. Gentry families.

PAGE 3
Lines 8-15. *The Laws of the Stannaries of Cornwall* (1808) Joseph Tregoning (J.T.) p.74 Gives the eight Blackmoor Tithings as:
Trethevy (Lanlivery or St. Austell); Boswith (Luxulyan); Treverbin (St Austell); Pridis (Luxulyan); Trenance Austle (St. Austell); Tremedris (Roche); Tregarrack (Roche) and Miliack (St Dennis). See P.A.S. Pool JRIC New Series vol. viii, part 4 (1981), pp.275-337.
Line 16. xxxviijs.ivd. = 38s.4d.
Line 29. Hallew alias Haledew. There are no capitals in original.
Line 40. vijs.viijd. = 7s.8d.

PAGE 4
Line 17. Triwarnhaile = Tywarnhaile.
Line 18. p'quisets = prerequisites.
Line 23. pretie bredth = pretty breadth. Quite broad.
Lines 21-25. The Tinners Common Seal. An early 14th century lead stannary seal for Cornwall was found in 1842 at Lee Down, Bath. It answers to the description above, with two tinners working with spade and pick. It has the legend: 'S' Comunatis Stangnatorum Cornubie' (Seal of the Community of Cornish Tinners). R.D. Penhallurick *Tin in Antiquity* (London 1986) p.244.
Line 10 onwards. Note Beare's argument for the ascendancy of Blackmore Stannary as the original grantees of Edward I's Charter.
Lines 27-29. See Pool (JRIC 1981) p.286. on tithings.

PAGE 5
Line 23. dimission = ? relinqishing/submission.
This page and to line 25 on page 6 deals with the Brokehouse Case.
See G.R. Lewis *The Stannaries* (Harvard 1908) pp.213, 215;
State Papers Domestic Mary iv.5.

PAGE 6
Line 1. stept = stopped ?

Line 2.   Coliers = charcoal burners or sellers.
Line 3.   cole = charcoal.
Line 16. Dec 18 1553.
Line 27. poyet = poet.
Line 36. In margin it has 'finer' (refiner).

PAGE 7
Lines 19, 25 & 29.   Spalier = the tinworker who serves to avoid a partner in the tinwork being being 'spaled' (fined) for absence. A wage earning labourer.

PAGE 8
Lines 32, 33 (and P.10 lines 30, 31) Thomas Beare recalled a time in the latter days of Henry VIII, circa 1546, when he was present at Truro as Bailiff of Blackmoor. Beare must have been a mature adult to hold this responsible position, one which required experience. His presence there in the late 1540s suggests that he was born at least as early of 1510-20.
Line 34. ma'tie = majesty.

PAGE 9
Line 17 etc.   Sir John Arundell of Trerise. See A.L. Rowse *Tudor Cornwall* on Arundell family. For comments on Bascawen v Caplin case see G.R. Lewis *The Stannaries* (Harvard 1908) pp.98, 99, 106, 110.

PAGE 10
Lines 11 & 12.   animatid. Animated = encouraged or inspired.
Lines 30 & 31.   'the writer hereof being bayliffe'. See footnote p.8.
Lines 26-34.   The case was heard before the Underwarden for the whole Stannary of Cornwall. Twenty-four jurors were picked from Blackmore Stannary, instead of the four stannaries each sending six men to make up the jury panel of 24 tinners. (Lewis p.110).
Line 34. hit = it.

PAGE 11
Lines 4 & 5.   Part of these two lines was originally in the margin and had to be added into the text to make sense.
Line 21. list = like/wish.

PAGE 12
Line 16. boll = bowl.
Line 21. iornies = jornies/journeys.
Line 29. Richard David given on page 13 as Richard (Ricus) Davye (Davy).
Line 29. Cramborne given elsewhere as Camborne.
Line 32. p'sequutid = prosecuted.

PAGE 13
Line 22. perches. Perch could vary between 9 and 26 feet as a linear measurement, although it became standardised at 16 ft. 6 inches.
J. Richardson (*The Local Historian's Encyclopedia.* (New Barnet, 1974) p.11; J.A. Buckley *Tudor Tinbounds* (Redruth 1988) p.18.

PAGE 16
Lines 14, 15.   Latin translation found in lines 15-17.
Line 17. throughly = thoroughly.
Line 18. p'swaded = persuaded.

Lines 21, 22. crave at end of line 21 repeated start of 22.
Line 32. In margin beside this line is the word 'Broad'.

PAGE 17
Line 4. happely = Happly/perhaps.
Line 12, etc. Gilbert Brokehouse. See Lewis 213, 214.

PAGE 18
Line 8. seal could be seas.
Line 8. ure = error.
Line 16. that = those.
Lines 18 & 19. thallegacons = the allegations.
Line 25. Condican = condition.
Line 32. r'yall = royal.
Line 35. bying = buying.

PAGE 19
Line 36 to line 25 on page 23. See *Lewis* pp.239-241 for his version. For Latin text throughout compare rendering with that of Thomas Pearce *Law & Customs of the Stanneries of the Counties of Cornwall and Devon* (2 parts) (1725).

PAGE 20
Line 27. 'emere bustam ad facturam' stanni…' 'to buy a grove/gear to make tin…' Or possibly buscum/boscum = wood. 'to buy wood' as smelting fuel. See Stannary Charter of 1201 (John) Lewis App.B p.238 & 1305 Charter (Edward I) App.D p.240.

PAGE 21
Line 7. 'hactemis' text quite clear on this word — what does it mean?

PAGE 22
Line 4. St. Michael's Day. Michaelmas. September 29th. Quarter day in England.

PAGE 24
Lines 2, 12. quite = quit.
Line 9. 'land, liffe or lym'. Land, life or limb.
Line 10. dep't = depart.
Line 10, 11. somons = summons.
Line 13. tallages. Feudal tax raised by king or lords from tenants.
          Tolles. Tax for liberty to use bridge/road or sell goods in market.
          Stallages. Rent for liberty to erect a market stall.
          Aydes. Aids. Feudal tax raised for specific or special purpose.
Lines 22 & 23. bushement. Wood as fuel for the hearth.
Line 28. growning = groaning. 'al pleas growning' = all pleas at issue/disputed.

PAGE 25
Line 8. thenquiry = the enquiry.
Line 10. thother = the other.
Line 16. cattle/cattles = chattels/chattels.
Line 20. Oyer. A hearing in a law court: 'oyer & terminer' means to hear & determine.
Lines 24, 25, 32. wayhed/wayhes/wayed = weighed/weights.

PAGE 26
Line 3. straighly = straightly. Immediately.

Line 11.   Saru'/Sarum = Salisbury. Carlishe = Carlisle.
Line 17.   xxxiijth year of Edward I was 1305.
Line 22.   cockels. Cockle = cornfield weed.
Line 22.   evers = weeds.
Line 24.   Call. Pryce (1778) says its a kind of ironstone found in gossan which impoverishes the lode. Possible manganese or wolfram.
           mundick. Whitish brittle ore with sulphide/pyrite.
           dare. Waste material.
           gard. Rough sand from tinwork.
           All four are waste materials to the tinner.
Line 30.   hatchwork. In this context same or similar to streamwork.
Lines 32, 33.   hayned/haine. Enclosed/enclose. Possibly from O.N. *Heqna* (Chambers).
Line 37.   fet. Obsolete English word for fetch.

PAGE 27
Lines 1, 18, 25 & 28.   Yoa. Tinners word for river. Yeo as place name element in Devon refers to a river or stream. Yeo, Yeau and Yeaw name of several rivers and brooks in Devon and signifies water. See W. Chapple *A Review of Part of Risden's Survey of Devon* (1785) (Barnstaple 1970) pp.60, 61.
Lines 12, 13.   Marishe. Old English word for marsh.
Line 24.   to weet. To wit. As follows, etc.
Lines 26, 29.   Cundite. Condite is local word for conduit/channel.
Lines 29, 30, 33.   tuele/*tutela* appears to mean 'to fence in'.
Lines 16, 32, 37.   bye leat/by leate. By leat can either be a by-pass leat, or a leat that runs alongside another leat or alongide a river. A leat is an artificial or man-made watercourse or gutter.

PAGE 28
Line 5.   abrode = abroad.
Lines 14, 28.   bonds = bounds.
Line 21.   list. Wish/like.

PAGE 29
Line 2.   fet = fetch.
Line 5.   farme. Lease.
Line 18 etc.   bond(s) = Bound(s).
Line 18.   meet. Obsolete word for measure.
Line 33.   Customers. Those subject to the customs of Blackmore.
Lines 25-30.   Marginal gloss: "can never be saved but only by pitching nue bonds round about for say they a work being once lost."

PAGE 30
Lines 25, 34.   haine = enclosure.
Line 26.   toll tyn. Proportion of black tin to bound owner or mineral lord.

PAGE 31
Line 2.   broder = broader/wider.
Line 3.   List = wish/like.
Lines 22-36.   Translation of bounds registration on lines 22-36. 'Blackmoor Stannary. Tinwork called St Agnes Beame alias Holy Roodwork (pre-Reformation name). To the aforesaid court held at Lostwithiel 12th April in the 20th year of the reign of our Lady Elizabeth by the Grace of God of England France & Ireland Queen Defender of the Faith, etc, came John Dinham, Nicholas Stanway and Peter Nance and they say that they have bounded a tinwork aforesaid on 6th March in the year aforesaid,

the bounds beginning on the east part with the course of Pasle Poole on the south part with the tinwork called Wellicaugh (from here on p.32) on the west part with the bounds of the tinwork called Goodluck and in the north part with the common highway of our lady Queen leading from the town of Austell towards Grampound just as the bounds and the limits in that place they have themselves.''

PAGE 32
Line 11.   othe = oath.
Lines 17-21.   l're = letter.
Line 20.   relistion. Relistion tin mine in Gwinear was working in the late-Medieval period. Its ore was unusual and complex. Possibly some of its constituants made it difficult to concentrate without contamination, resulting in black tin that was difficult to smelt. Hence, its reputation for hardness.
Lines 31, 35.   amerciaments/amarcements. Fines. Discretionary fine/punishment.

PAGE 33
Lines 15, 17, 23.   lost/losts = loss/losses.

PAGE 34
Line 28.   conningst = cunningest.
Line 16, 38 etc.   lost = loss.

PAGE 35
Lines 2, 9, 37.   mett/meet/meat/meater = measure/measures/measurer.
Lines 5-13.   4 quarts = 1 foot.
　　　　　　1 foot = 5 gallons & 1 pottle (Winchester).
　　　　　　1 quart = 2 quarts & 1 pint (Winchester).
Line 6.   Foot fate. See Lewis p.171.
Line 34.   ashoring = assuring.

PAGE 36
Lines 10, 11, 16, 40.   mett/meating. Measured/measuring.
Line 16.   this = thus.
Line 25.   vd.ob = 5½d.
Line 28.   xxv li = £25.
Line 29.   xvs.vijd.ob = 15s.7½d.
Line 33.   xixs.vjd.quarta = 19s.6¼d.
Line 37.   chevest = chiefest.

PAGE 37
Lines 4, 5.   lost/losts = loss/losses.
Line 10.   mocion = motion.
Lines 15, 19, 21, etc.   m'sters/m'rs = masters.
Line 13.   y̆ = those.
Line 21.   conag = coinage.
Line 30.   Coliers = charcoal burners. Cole/coale = charcoal.
Line 30, 31, 33.   Cole Chariers. Charcoal was carried from the burning places to the blowing houses on pack horses, mules and ponies, large numbers of which were employed. The twice yearly tin blowing periods used vast quantities of charcoal.

PAGE 38
Lines 1, 2.   Distance charcoal brought to Blackmore was 30 to 40 miles which could be from well into Devon.
Lines 8-18.   Charcoal measured by volume.   1 pack   = 3 bushells

20 gallons	= 1 bushell
1 bushell	= 1 hogshead
1 hogshead	= 1 Bordeaux Cask

All measurements varied over the centuries and have represented different weights or volumes for different produce, i.e.

Hogshead: 52.5 Imperial galls. of beer.
             54 Imperial galls. of claret.
             46 Imperial galls. of tobacco.

Line 21. empt = empty.
Lines 28, 38. toller. Appears to be a stannary official rather than a mineral lord's employee. He was here deputising for the bailiff.

PAGE 39
Lines 25, 33. hower = hour.
Line 36. meating. Measuring.

PAGE 40
Line 10. maine prison. The Lostwithiel gaol.
Lines 11-13. The time of writing. 1586.
Lines 18, etc. keep = keeper.
Line 22. iijd. = 3d. or iiijd. = 4d.
Line 25. list = wishes/likes.
Line 26. kepe = keeper.
Line 33. frinds = friends.

PAGE 41
Lines 1, 4. keep = keeper(s).
Line 10. p'secute = prosecute.
Lines 10, 33. accion/accon = action.
Line 20. tharchangle = the archangel.

PAGE 42
Line 20. Latin *querens*. Translated 'querent' in the sense of litigant or petitioner.

PAGE 43
Line 1. p't = plaintiff.
Line 3 etc. *replevin*. Used from the 15th cent. From Anglo-French & Old French 'replevir'. Legal term referring to the recovery of goods unlawfully taken. Writ of repleven to establish ownership of goods and restore to legal owner.
Line 6. ther = their.
Line 7. L. = Lord.
Line 14. Q.m'tie = Queens majesty.

PAGE 44
Line 6. stick = scruple.
Line 7. gent = gentlemen.
Line 8. lawier = lawyer.
Line 17. xx li. = £20.
Line 20. *fyeri facias*. Fieri facias. Used from 15th century. Legal term for writ ordering a levy on the goods of a debter.
Lines 22, 24. Nichill/nichels. See lines 9-15 on page 45.
Lines 23, 32, 34. *distringas*. From the Latin 'you shall distrain'. Legal term. Formerly a writ ordering a sheriff to act.
Line 27. def = defendant.

Line 27. pl = plaint.
Line 27. Last word on line unclear. Could be 'denad' or 'denied'.
Line 30. plent = complaint/complent.
Line 35. pl = plaintiff.

PAGE 45
Line 4. *alias distringas*. Another distringas. Footnote page 44.
Lines 4 & 5. *plures distringas*. A further distrangas.
Line 6. amercement. Fine.
Line 6. di'str = distress or *distringas*.
Line 13, etc. write = writ.
Line 19, etc. p'cess = ?process
Line 27, etc. pl = plaintiff/plaint.

PAGE 46
Line 2. pl = plaintiff.
Line 5. lyvying = levying.
Line 6. *fieri facias*. Writ commanding sheriff to distrain goods.
Line 12. *Distringas*. See footnote p.44.
Line 14. adnihiled = annihilated/made void.
Line 15. wryte = writ.

PAGE 48
Line 29. 'mention is made before pag' = Mention is made on an earlier page.
Line 31. L. = Lord.
Line 39. mellor. Either English miller or Cornish 'melynor' (miller). The mill would have been either a stamping mill or a crasing mill.

PAGE 49
Line 8. ijd. = 2d.

PAGE 50
Lines 1, 5. pyners/p'oners. Pioneers/sappers/diggers, etc.
Line 11. Word 'tynners' appears to have been changed from 'tynnworks'.
Lines 14, 18, 23, etc. Captaines. Shows term used generally in tinworks & not just in mines that are supposed to have been influenced by Germans. Honorary title captain used in England throughout Medieval times for leader in industry, army, navy, religion and mines.
Lines 27, 30. seised/seased. Seize, as in possession of.
Line 29. avoyded. Dispossessed.
Line 38. paine. ? Punishment.

PAGE 52
Line 2. ple'tyve = plaintiff.
Line 6. whereas = whereof.
Line 24. lyvery = delivery.
Lines 26, 30. Appellacons. Latin 'appelatus' to appeal.

PAGE 53
Line 1. onward. Case of Trewennard v. Reskarrack see Lewis pp.112, 114.
Line 3. xxixth. = 29th.
Line 21. Q. bence = Queen's bench.
Line 27. Scaddion or Scadion.

PAGE 54
Line 11. p'sequuting = prosecuting.
Line 11. thintent = the intent.
Line 32. sursease = sure seize.
Line 39. averse = oppose. Latin *aversus* 'to turn away from'.

PAGE 55
Line 15. then = than.
Lines 16, 38, etc. cattle. Probably chattel(s) but could be cattle.
Line 16. compli' = complainant.
Line 28. 'adheere'. The first two letters are not clear, although the 'd' appears certain.
Lines 35-37. Stannary Charters, etc, ratified by Act of Parliament.

PAGE 56
Line 29. chance. J. Hatcher *English Tin Production & Trade Before 1550* (Oxford 1973) p.65
          gives this as 'change'. The letter is certainly 'c'.
Line 39. 'agitum serum' Douch gives ?'miserum'. However, agitum appears clear enough,
          although 'serum' could be 'serund' or similar.
Lines 30, 34, 35. farmers/farmour. Hatcher calls farmers tributors (p.67).

PAGE 57
Line 34. then = than.
Pages 57 and 58 contain a fine description of tinners charity toward the poor among them.
Lines 33, 34. Gives informative list of tinners food. Bread, dairy products (butter & cheese)
          and meat (beef, pork & bacon).
Line 23. Beare does not say what was in the tinners drink bottle.

PAGE 58
Line 3.   Xt = Christ.
Line 4.   furnessed = furnished.
Lines 2, 3. A gloss in the margin gives Luk(e) 21 & Mark 12.
Line 8.   intring = entering.
Line 17-35. captaine. How did the arrangement work? Was he captain of one set of bounds
          or of the group of bounds on a particular moor or bal?
Line 23. 'quatched' = scratched.
Lines 25, 33. lacking/lacker/lacke. Absent/absentee.

PAGE 59
Line 6.   sempelst = simplest.
Line 10. aquavite. A preservative. Probably *aqua vite* 'water of life', i.e. brandy.
Line 22. pickes = picks.
Line 24. 'brewes' is probably 'brawse/brawes' as line 38. Brawse appears to be stones/pebbles
          in the alluvium as opposed to the sand and slime. These stones required stamping to
          reduce them for washing in the buddles.
Line 27. iij li = £3.
Line 27. five markes. A mark was worth 8oz of silver. A pound was 16oz. An oz. of silver
          was worth 20 pence (1s. 8d.) and 8oz. were worth 160 pence (13s. 4d.). Five marks
          were worth £3.6.8d.

PAGE 60
Line 31. ther = their.
Line 34. recriat = recreate.
Line 36. blont = blunt.

PAGE 62
Line 3. cleaneweried = exhausted.
Line 6. as = is.
Line 6. husband man. A working farmer. One who works his own land or his rented land.
Line 7. happely/happly = perhaps.
Line 25. deafe stones. Barren, valueless stones.

PAGE 63
Line 34. cuningst = cunningest.

PAGE 64
Line 17. L. = Lord.
Line 36. M̄ = £1,000.

PAGE 65
Line 8. vd. iiijd.ob. iiijd = 5d, 4½d. & 4d.
Line 10. loe = low.
Line 20. rekninges = reckonings.
Line 24. xx li. = £20. xxvij li = £27.
Line 26. ob. = ½d.
Line 27. vd.ob. = 5½d.
Line 30. iiijd.ob. = 4½d.
Line 31. xxiiij li. = £24.
Line 31. guyd = guide.
Line 32. M li. = £1,000.
Line 33. iiijd.ob. = 4½d.
Line 33. xiijs.vid. = 13s.6d.

PAGE 66
This table is an early — possibly the earliest — 'tin table' that enabled tinners to relate quickly the values of different qualities of assayed ore. Given as so many pence per marke they could ascertain the price they would expect to get per foot of tin stuff, the 1000 weight being worth £20, £21, etc. B. Earl.

PAGE 67
Line 14. iustice = justice.
Line 18. m = master.
Line 19. ? Cilsan.
Line 20. lete court = court leet. Usually a manorial court that met twice a year and dealt with petty offences and the election of minor, local officials.
Line 21. lutin or luta.
Line 31. thessise = the assize.
Line 33. bolles = bowls.
Lines 31, 34, etc. Do us to weet (to wit) = cause us to know (inform us) Chambers Dictionary p.1499.

PAGE 68
Line 2. doble = double.
Lines 17 & 19. stolne/st'lne = stolen.
Line 20. viij tuthings = 8 tithings.
Line 24. Q.Ma'tie = Queen's Majesty.
Line 28. tharchangle = the archangel.
Line 30. 'shall enquire' crossed out.
Line 33. thaccustomed = the accustomed.

PAGE 69
Lines 3 & 12. crossed out words.
Line 4.   lostes = losses.
Line 7.   othe = oath.
Line 13.   tuthinmen = tithingmen.
Lines 24 & 34. kep/keps/underkeep = keeper/keepers/underkeeper.

PAGE 70
Line 13.   corerse = course.
Line 13.   strayted. Restricted/narrowed.
Line 15.   fet = fetch.
Line 21.   fetteth = fetcheth.
Lines 33 & 34. thintent = the intent.
Line 34 & 35, etc. 'do us to weet (wit)' = cause us to know, etc.

PAGE 71
Lines 13 & 29. 'do us to weet (wit)' see above.
Line 31.   maior = mayor.
Line 32.   tolsill = tolsell/tolsey. Local name for toll office. Chambers p.1359.

PAGE 72
Line 3.   auctorised = authorised.
Line 26.   'quirting up the river' means silting up the river.
Line 29.   L. = Lord.
Line 32.   xiijth = 13th.
Line 33.   m'ts = majesties.
Line 34.   iiij = 4.

PAGE 73
Line 5.   v li = £5.
Line 6.   *fieri facias* A writ commanding a sheriff to distrain goods.
Line 7.   m'te = majesty.
Line 15.   xxvijth = 27th.
Line 15.   xiijth = 13th.
Lines 20 & 21. L. = Lord.
Lines 23 & 24. Q.ma'ts = Queen's majesty.
Line 25.   'it is enacted' is crossed out.
Line 30.   Westm' = Westminster.
Line 30.   xxijth = 22nd.
Line 31.   xxvijth = 27th.

PAGE 74
Line 4.   'wthin' crossed out because it is repeated on line 5.
Line 27.   farthr = further.

PAGE 75
Line 1.   'xij men or moe' = 12 men or more.
Line 5.   xl = 40.
Line 6.   cattals = chattels.
Line 10.   thother = the other.
Line 12.   ? sstsoones.
Lines 17, 19. moytie = moiety. Half.
Line 21.   essyne. Essoin/essoyn = excuse for not appearing in court. Used in Spencer (Chambers).
Line 22.   'wager of law'. Pledge or oath in legal language (Chambers).

Line 29. maineprise. Surety, especially for appearance of prisoners (Chambers).

PAGE 76
Line 1. v li = £5.
line 2. *fieri facias*. See footnote p.73.
Line 10. grownes = grounds?
Line 15. 'throughly wrought unto the shelfe'. Shelf = bedrock/rockhead.
Line 29 & 30. abudance = abundance.
Lines 30 & 31. 'in the noysance' = to the nuisance.
Line 33. asseised = assessed?
Line 36. Last word crossed out.

PAGE 77
Line 2. ffects = facts.
Line 23. Tresulian alias Kern. This family, which held land, in, among other places, Illogan (Trevenson) was also called Tresillian alias Keene or Carne.

PAGE 78
Line 14. darkest = obscurest.
Line 15. straiting = restricting.
Line 21. exposion = exposition.

PAGE 81
Line 14. Pearce (1725) gives £15 instead of £40.
Lines 26, 29. several. Enclosed land.

PAGE 82
Apart from lines 35, 36 the whole page translated from Latin.

PAGE 87
Line 1. def' = defendant.
Line 6. ylles = ills.
Line 12. accon = action.
Lines 14-20. Mostly Latin translated into English.
Line 26. 'In this present 1586'. Date of writing.
Line 27. coop'tners = copartners.
Line 33. xvij or xviij = 17 or 18 doles. The xvij is smudged and the margin has '16'.

PAGE 88
Line 10. reneuing = renewing.
Line 13, 20, 23, etc. bonding/bonds/bownes = bounding/bounds.
Line 28. this = thus.

PAGE 89
Line 1. quarrle = quarrel.
Line 20. ploclamacon = proclamation.
Line 29. C li = £100.
Line 29. p'testacon = protestacon.

PAGE 90
Line 11. Somewhat = something.
Line 22. pl ? Plaintiff?
Line 23. Latin.
Line 26. avoid = remove.
Line 30. Latin.

PAGE 91
Line 4.   Awdite = audit.

PAGE 92
Line 1 & 2. lost/losts = loss/losses.
Line 4.   l'rs = letters.
Line 5.   meat = measures.
Line 16.   Cawle = coal.
Line 17.   hower = hour.

PAGE 93
Lines 1, 6, 8, 18, etc.   See footnotes on *repleven*, *nichill* (nihill), *fieri facias*, *distringas* and
                           appellation. pp.44, 45, 73.
Line 14.   avoyded. Removed.
Line 20.   write = writ.
Line 23.   Number 56 was written 53 in error.
Line 27.   Number 60 appears to be 64, but refers to page 60.

PAGE 94
Line 9.   xiiij(14) or xviij(13).
Line 11.   v li = £5.
Line 18.   several lands. Enclosed lands.

PAGE 95
Lines 10 & 12 etc.   meating/meat, etc = measureing/measure, etc.
Line 32.   light met = light measure.
Line 34.   abate = lessen/reduce.

PAGE 96
Line 4.   theris = theirs.
Line 8.   list = wish.
Line 9.   ffower = four.
See R. Carew *The Survey of Cornwall* (1602) ed. F.E. Halliday (New York 1969) p.96 on
measurements/weights of tin.

PAGE 97
Line 18 & 20.   'Noyes fflood'/'Noyes flood' = Noah's flood.
                 See Carew (1602) ed. Halliday (1969) pp.88, 89; Genesis chs. 6-8.

PAGE 98
Line 21.   frence = French.
Lines 30-34. in 14th century French. Untranslated.

PAGE 99
From line 30 on page 98 to line 27 page 99, the 14th century French of the Parliamentary Roll
has been left untranslated.

PAGE 100
Line 27.   adnull = nullify.

PAGE 101
Line 10.   p'fyt = perfyt/perfect.
Line 12.   '36 yere past' i.e. c.1550.
Line 13.   In margin beside: 'Brawd'.

Lines 25, 26.   In margin beside: 'rux'.
Line 34.   xxvjs.viijd. = 26s.8d.

PAGE 102
Line 1.   Before David, Robt & Richard was crossed out.
Line 4.   John Vanston. This could be a Dutch name or a corruption of the Cornish surname
Vincent/Vencent.
Line 5.   Burdiaux = Bordeaux.
Line 33.   casualties. Obsolete term for tailings or by products of tin dressing. Gangue material.

PAGE 103
Line 12.   thone = the one.
Line 13.   Q. m'ties = Queen's majesties

PAGE 104
Lines 1-22.   Assay by the shovel (later called the vanning trial) as well as the use of a wet hand
to determine the value of an ore are noted in some length. Such knowledge appears
to be only imperfectly understood by present day researchers and Thomas Beare's
account is a unique source of reliable information. B. Earl
Line 8.   p'fyter = perfyter/perfect.
Lines 10, 11, 12 & 15.   weat/weate = wet.
Line 16.   were as = whereas.
Line 25.   god = good.
Lines 27, 29.   waying = weighing.
Line 29.   60 li. = 60lb.
Line 29.   4d.ob. = 4½d.
Line 30.   50 li. = 50lb.
Line 32.   2 li. - 2lb.
Line 35.   2d.ob. = 2½d.

PAGE 105
Lines 11, 23 & 33.   lost/losts = loss/losses.
Line 12.   thoth'r = the other.
Line 17.   'light measure after the custome of Blackmoor'. This 'light' 12 foot measure, which
was customarily used in Blackmoor, meant that they probably poured the black tin
into the container without packing it, or possibly it was filled level rather than heaped.
B. Earl
Line 20.   'house hath bin cold'. Beare commented that blowing tin in a blowinghouse that had
not reached and stabilised out a steady heat did not produce the best results. My own
experiments confirm that a furnace needs to be hot before blowing starts and then should
be maintained at a stable temperature. B. Earl

Line 24.   Saphick verses. Four line verses said to have been invented by Sappho (c.600 BC Greek
lyric poetess).
Line 26.   sent = scent.
Line 27.   they = thy.
Line 33.   profe = proof.

PAGE 106
Lines 1-31.   Beare describes how the tin dresser preparing the black tin for blowing must treat
each type of material differently. The stream tin and mine tin should be kept separate
as they need to be dealt with differently by the blower. Also, the coarser moor tin
must be kept separate from the fine moor tin for the same reason.
Beare had s skillful tinner separate the mixed material into ideal sizes, so that

the best results would be obtained. The tinner did this at a buddle in or close to the blowinghouse. He used water at differnt velocities to classify the pulp into different sizes. The two coarser grades were separated on the buddle and the fine grade was caught in a linen cloth at the discharge. The light waste was carried over the cloth as failings. Such classifying or ore pulp during dressing is indicative of highly skilled workmanship. B. Earl

Line 3.   xiijtine = 13.
Line 6.   a sonder = asunder/apart.
Line 9.   suter = suiter.
Line 14.   p'fycte = perfect.
Lines 14 & 33.   heat/hote = hot.
Lines 24 & 26.   small = fine.
Line 25.   abating = reducing.
Line 27.   britch = breech.
Line 28.   lincloth = linencloth.
Lines 31-35.   The blower ensured that his hearth/furnace was fully heated and in good order before any of the separated lots of black tin were blown. B. Earl
Line 33.   p'fyt = perfect.

PAGE 107
Lines 1, 2.   consequently = subsequently i.e. next.
Line 4.   p'fyt = perfect.
Line 20.   408 li. = 408lb.
Lines 7-35.   The text appears to indicate that although good tin appeared in the float, the best white tin metal yield occured in the 'sinders' (slag); indeed Beare seems to say the best tin metal is in the slag. All this indicates slag crushing with metal separation, probably by buddle, was an important part of the tin blowing process. If this is so, it corresponds well with the indications coming out with the study of pre- 2500 BC Turkish tin smelting.
Beare obtained a yield of 408 lb. in total of tin metal from his 13 foot of black tin concentrates.
Time is well spent in buddling the various natures of ore to a high grade in order to avoid undue losses in the smelting. B. Earl

PAGE 108
Lines 6-10.   The nature of the noise of the blast from the nozzles in the furnace gives a good indication of the state of working of the furnace. (This was also my experience). B. Earl
Line 9.   falt = fault.
Line 12.   britche = breech.
Line 12.   "Two feet in the britche": this probably indicates the width of the bellows (or their size). B. Earl
Line 14.   xiiij inches = 14 inches.
Lines 14-23.   The nozzle entrance hole in the side of the furnace should be fourteen inches above the bottom discharge hole through which the molten tin flows out of the furnace into the float — a groove cut in a stone which took the tin from the furnace and from which the tin was ladled into the mould. If the holes were too close the base of the hearth would be melted out (this was also my experience). Nozzle is the Cornish term for what, elsewhere, is called a 'tuyere'.
With smaller bellows: ten or twelve inches between the holes should be used for efficient work, otherwise "ten pounds or more tin will be lost": presumably from a thirteen foot charge. B. Earl
Line 22.   xls. = 40s.
Line 24.   meating = measuring.

Line 31.   xxxv li. = £35.
Line 34.   prove = proof.

PAGE 109
Line 1.   lx li. = 60lb.
Line 5.   cv li = 105lb.
Lines 5 & 9.   met = measure.
Line 6.   'tharchangle' = the archangel.
Line 11.   v li. = 5lb.
Line 15.   Q. m't = Queen's majesty's.
Line 25.   tine = tin.
Line 26.   p'ties = parties. Foreign parts.
Lines 32 & 33.   losts = losses.

PAGE 110
Line 7.   other = even.
Lines 3, 8, etc.   m'rs = masters.

PAGE 111
Line 20.   meting = measuring.

INDEX

Bridge, Lostwithiel 72
Broad plates (lead) 5
Broadface (owl) 63
Brokehouse, Gilbert 5 6 17 18 48
Brother of tinner 59 88
Brother, Queens 5
Buddle money 60 101
Buddle place 106
Buddle(s) 5 59 74 97
Buddle, breach of 106
Bushel 38 69
Bushment 24
Butter 57
Buyers 8 11 17 18 35-37 59 65 104 109
   110
Bye leat 27

Call 26
Camborne 12 13
Canterbury 98
Caplin, John 9-11
Captain owners of tinworks 53
Captains of tinworks 58 60
Carlisle, John, Bishop of 22 26
Carpenter(s) 8
Carriers, coal 37
Caske, Bordeaux 38
Casting 8
Castle Park (Lostwithiel) 101
Castle, Restormel 72
Casualties (by-products) 102
Cat(s) 63 64
Causes (disputes) 2
Certificate 48 49
Chafe (chaff) 26
Chancellor 19
Chancellor, Lord 6
Charge(s)/Charged 4 12 97
Charges (costs) of tinwork 60 97
Charges of Stannary Court 67
Charitable orders 59
Charity 57 59 60
Charter(s) 2-5 8 11 12 19 23 48 54 55 77
   78 98 100 103 109
Chattel(s) (Chatell/Cattle) 25 55 75
Cheese 57
Cherished, the sick 59
Chester, Earl of (Richard) 98
Chevender 13 14
Chief bailiff 64
Chief customers 40
Chief steward 10
Chief warden 71 90
Chigwin, John 77

Child/children 57 59 88
Christ, Saviour 67
Christians 67
Churchyards 12
Cicero 67
Cities 1
Claimers of bounds 90
Claims against costs 60
Cleansed tin 12 26 59 96 106 107
Clothing 57
Coal (charcoal) 6 37-39 69
Coal burners 37
Coal carriers 37
Coal packs 38 69
Cockels 26
Coffer 4
Coin(ed) 25 71 109
Coinage 5 8-11 37 39 58 59 69 70 109
Coinage, common 109
Coinage, post 109
Cold blowinghouse 105
Collection 3 48 49
Colliers 6 37 38 69
Collins, Thomas 77
Command(s) 25 26
Commissioners 73
Commit offence 25
Commodity 19
Common griefs 4
Common right 100
Commons 38
Common seal 4
Commonwealth 71
Company of rulers 11
Company of tinners 11 58-60 87 88
Company, new 88
Complainant 55
Complaint, bill of 56
Conduit 27
Conference 49
Confession 74
Constable 48 49
Contempt 54
Contract(s) 24
Controllers 11
Controversy 10 11
Convey (water) 12
Convicted 75
Copartners 50 87 88
Copy of decree 6 17
Cord 29 61 74 87
Corn 26
Corner (bounds) 27-29
Cornes (tin) 101

Precinct 2
Predis 3
Premises 12
Prerequisites 4
Prerogative 2 5
Prerogative, Royal (preemption) 103
Preservative 59
Price (of black tin) 65 104
Price (of tin) 5 109
Price, common 64 65
Price making (white tin) 64
Price, high 9
Prideaux 2
Prince 2-8 12 13 17 44 49 52 71 78
Prince's Council 71 78
Principal tinner 8
Priors 23 24
Prison 25 40 75
Prisoner(s) 40 64 69 70 75
Prisoners (poor/gentlemen) 40
Prisoners at large in town (surety) 40
Prisoners charged/kept/payed for by friends
    40 41
Privilege 8
Privy Council 18 52 56
Process 34
Proclamation(s) 31 88 90
Procurements 54
Profit 1 56
Profit divided 60
Prosecuted 12 41
Proverb, Saphick 105
Provosts 23
Purchasers (of Charter) 4
Purgeth, wind 26
Purified/purify (tin) 6 12 26 59 60 95-97
    101 103 106
Pyder, Hundred 3

Quarrel 89
Quart fate 35
Quart measure 35 36 95 96 109
Quart, true (Winchester Measure) 35 68
Queen 8 18 34 40 43 49 68 70-73 75 76
    87 103
Queen Mary 6
Queen's bench 53
Queen's brother 5
Queen's exchequer 3
Queen's hammer 39 109
Queen's house 9
Queen's palace 6 19
Quirting 72
Quittance(s) 26

Quoynage (coynage) 5 49

Raleigh, Sir Walter 46 47
Rat(s) 63 64
Rate/rated 64
Ratement 49
Reader, the 6
Realm (England) 1
Receiver, Master (of Cornwall) 49
Receivership, office of 9
Record(s) 12 64
Records, ancient 11
Recreation 60
Refines (fineth) 26
Reformation of enormities etc 67
Relief (of poor) 58
Relistion tin mark 'R' 32 33 69
Renewing day 29 88
Renould 2
Rent 57
Replevin 43
Restormel Castle 72
Reydon, Thomas 5
Rich tinners 57
Richard II 78 98 100
Right of tinwork inherited 48
Right, work his 7
Rishe 27
River 26 27 63 74
Rivers, great 72 76
Roche 2
Rochester, Bishop of 6
Rochester, Robert 19
Rock(s) 97
Rod or goad 58
Roll, Parliamentary 101
Romans 67
Rooker (cat) 63 64
Roskarrack, John (Reskarrock) 53 55
Round bounds 29
Rubble 72 74 76
Rulers 11 78
Russell, Lord (Chief Warden) 90
Rux 59 101

Sale of tin 5 9 110
Sale of tin abroad 33
Salvation 67
Sanctuary (ground) 12
Sand(s) 72 76
Saphick proverb 105
Sarum 22
Sarum, Bishop of 26
Saviour Christ 58

Superior company 11
Supplication, tinners general 6
Surety 9 45 46
Sussex, Henry 19
Sussex, Lord of 6
Sute (suit) 2 3 5 6
Sward (grass) 27
Swine 68
Sworn 28 40

Table of Rating 65
Tackle 59
Tail (of work) 27 28
Tallages 24
Tamar River 76
Tapsters 67
Tavistock 72 73 77
Tayle (arse) 63
Tayler (tailor) 8
Tails (tayles) 29 30 72 89
Tailings (taylings) 30
Teignmouth 72
Testament 52
Testing quality of black tin 104
Three pounds 3
Tide (period of blowing/12 hours) 107
Tin brawse 62
Tin hatch 30
Tin hole (in hearth) 108
Tin makers 68
Tin marks 34
Tinbags 57
Tincourt (Tyncourt) 54
Tinner merchants 5 38
Tinnerlike treatise 60
Tinpits 76
Tinstones 59 62
Tithing men (eight) 3 69
Tithings/Tuthinges 2 3 4
Title to tyn work 59 70
Toll tin 30
Toll(s) 12 24
Tollage 71
Toller(s) 38-40 69 71
Tolsill 71
Tomyow 2
Tools 1
Tools, iron 1
Towel 63
Towns 1 5 24 25 71
Toy 60
Traine 28
Travel 60
Traveller(s) 12 69

Treasures 5
Treasury 58
Tregorreck (Tregarrack) 3
Tremodres 3
Trenance Austell 3
Trerise (Trerice) 9
Trespass 12 24 51 52 89
Trethewye 3
Treverbin 3
Trewinnard, George 53
Trewinnard, Martin (Trewaynnard) 53-55
Trial 10 70
Triangle bounds 29
Tribulage (shovell money) 3
Trinkell, softly 36
Trouble (for tinners) 7 8 12 17
Trounsen, John 77
Truro 8 9 21 25
Tried and sworn 11
Tuele 27 28
Turf 24 57
Turf, green (lay tin on) 40
Turning turves 27
Tutela 27
Tye(s) 74 87 89
Tywarnhaile/Triwarnhaile 4 14 77

Unblown 68
Underkeeper (of gaol) (underkeeper/deputy) 69
Undermined 12
Understeward 10 53
Underwarden 10 56 71 76
Unsealed measures 67
Usage 100
Userer 1

Vacant 27
Vacant ground 31 43 87 88
Valencia, Adam of 22 26
Valleys 97
Value of gold rings 101
Vanning with shovel (word vanning not used) 104
Vanston, John (merchant) 102
Verdict 17 75
Vice Warden 48 90
Victuals 57
Villages 25
Villains 24
Violence/violently 70 80
Virtue 67
Void work 29 88